CHINESE ANIMAL PAINTING MADE EASY

Rebecca Yue

BATSFORD

First published in the United Kingdom in 2009 by
Batsford
10 Southcombe Street
London
W14 0RA

An imprint of Anova Books Company Ltd

ISBN 978 1 9063 8850 8

A CIP catalogue record for this book is available from the British Library.

17 16 15 14 13 12 11 10 09
10 9 8 7 6 5 4 3 2 1

Reproduction by Mission Productions Ltd, Hong Kong
Printed and bound by 1010 Printing International Ltd, China

This book can be ordered direct from the publisher at the website
www.anovabooks.com, or try your local bookshop.

Page 2: Tigers are always favourite subjects for animal painting with
Chinese brushes.
Left: Zebras can be created using simple lines with ink and colours. The full
painting can be seen on page 164.
Page 6: For painting white animals, most artists prefer simply to draw the
outline and leave the body blank. I enjoy the challenge of painting it in
white. See page 146 for this painting step by step.

CH**ibraries**   Royal Kingston   AINTING

returned
Kingston
on or
date
f the item
y another
renewed
to a
e times by
nbership
ns issued
hree-week
enewable.

uk/libraries

ACKNOWLEDGEMENTS

I started writing this book at the beginning of 2007. However, this was to prove a year of mixed fortunes. The high note, of course, was the publication of my fourth book on Chinese art, *Chinese Landscapes Made Easy*, which was subsequently shortlisted for the 2007 Practical Art Instruction Book of the Year award. Shortly after that it was confirmed that I had cancer and so began the long and tough fight for my life. Let me take this opportunity to offer heartfelt thanks to my family, my pupils and all my friends around the world, who supported me through this difficult time.

There were good days and there were bad days. Continuing to work on this book enabled me to focus amid a sea of mixed emotions. Now, late in 2008, I have finished writing it. Also, my consultant has given me the all clear, so this book has become a celebration of a new chapter in my life.

I am very proud of this book and I hope you will be also.

Rebecca

CONTENTS

INTRODUCTION

As with all subjects found in Chinese brush painting, you can paint animals either with a detailed and elaborate outline style or with the expressive non-outline approach. In the ancient period, almost all paintings of animals were executed with the outline technique. This style emphasizes the details. Figures are drawn carefully: every detail is depicted in the outlines and layers of colours are applied one after another to create tones and depth. Artworks of this style are usually painted on Xuan paper or silk, sized with alum and gum to make them non-absorbent so that colours can be spread in a controlled way. The outline style remains popular among artists as a technique for painting animals.

The Chinese non-outline approach to painting animals became popular around a hundred years ago, so it is relatively modern compared with the outline style. However, the non-outline style has developed so rapidly over the last hundred years that it has come to dominate animal painting in modern times. 'Non-outline', by the way, does not mean that you cannot use lines in a painting. However, lines are used in a more flexible, expressive way than in the outline style. Another distinctive characteristic of the non-outline style is that Chinese brushes are manoeuvred to create brushstrokes. These brushstrokes form shapes, creating movements as well as tones.

Animals and people are usually subjects that come towards the end of an apprenticeship in Chinese brush painting. Many artists may never embark on this stage, deciding instead to specialize in other subjects, such as flowers and birds or landscapes. There are two types of animal painter. The first are those who follow a general training, briefly studying every subject featured in brush paintings. At the end of their training, if they decide to specialize in painting animals, each of them will seek to enrol with a master who has specialized in that subject. However, the majority of animal artists will already have become accomplished artists in other categories of Chinese brush painting before they eventually turn their full attention to painting animals. Each of the latter group will already have succeeded in developing his or her unique style, as well as polished techniques. When they apply these qualities to animal painting, they create a wide range of styles, combined with highly advanced techniques. Also, because they are accomplished artists, they are not afraid to stretch the brush to produce amazing new effects. As a consequence, it can be confusing and daunting for newcomers to Chinese brush painting who want to learn to paint animals and take these masters as their models.

Perhaps if we can understand how a master approaches painting an animal, we may find a way to follow their example. Actually, there is no real mystery here. We usually start with all the basic techniques at our disposal. We then experiment with all of them, combining, stretching and varying them, until we finally discover a form that we feel perfectly expresses our concept of the subject. Each artist has his or her own conception of an animal. The character, the movement, the location, and the relationship between each artist and animal are all different. So the outcome is significantly different from one

Opposite: The panda is a symbol of China and a must for the animal painter to try.

artist to another. It is also interesting to know that some masters prefer to paint all their animals using one technique, while many others choose to mix many techniques in their work.

Bearing this in mind, I have decided to guide my readers to think like accomplished artists. As with many areas of artistic endeavour, the key is to master the basic techniques. All through the book, before painting each animal, I shall demonstrate how to combine and vary basic techniques to form complex strokes with which to depict particular animals. And, in the course of learning, you will also embrace many of the more popular Chinese styles of painting animals.

The learning process begins with knowing the correct materials and equipment. Readers who have used my other books to learn aspects of Chinese brush painting will be familiar with the majority of items I have chosen to use here, but I shall list all of them again. In addition, I am introducing two new types of brush that are essential for effective animal painting, as explained here.

The first of these is a large brush. This is a very convenient tool for painting large shapes, such as the body of an animal, but you have to work on the press-and-lift technique a bit more if you are to create a shape successfully. Bear in mind that the original artworks in this book are much larger. We have had to size them down to fit into this book. So when you practise using the examples in this book, you can use the large brushes and work on a grand scale.

I also introduce you to a slender brush for painting the more delicate features of animals, such as the faces and the feet. People are usually attracted primarily to the expressive broad brushstrokes that characterize Chinese brush painting. Many might imagine that the non-outline way of painting animals would only use broad, expressive brushstrokes of this type. Contrary to what these people may think, detailed and delicate brushstrokes are equally attractive and just as essential to painting animals. Experienced artists always use a balance of the delicate as well as the broad brushstrokes to create a composition with many contrasts, showing the whole character of the animal. In fact, this principle applies to all subjects of brush painting. Detailed, delicate features will enhance an artwork made up of broad expressive brushstrokes because they highlight the beauty of the latter. The illustrations of this book will very much reflect this principle, so this slender brush will prove a useful and essential tool.

I am keeping the chapter of basic techniques very simple. I shall therefore not go into too many variations and combinations. The whole aim is to let you concentrate on getting the simple forms of the basic techniques right at the very beginning, so that when we come to use them later to develop the more complex forms, you will not feel hesitant. The session on 'Manoeuvring Chinese Brushes' (page 34) contains important information, particularly about using Chinese brushes for painting animals. I shall give you hints on using different sizes of brush, especially the very large one and the very slender one. Then there is the essential instruction on loading a brush so that you have the right amount of moisture. Painting animals requires a delicate balance of moisture in the brush. Moisture causes colours to run, so too much moisture often causes bleeding beyond the intended outline, resulting in a clumsy effect.

The wrist movement, elbow movement and press-and-lift techniques are fundamental to using a Chinese brush effectively. The brush is used on its side more with animal painting than with any other subject found in Chinese brush painting because this creates broader brushstrokes. There are several ways of using the brush on its side, as I shall explain. Dry brushwork and wet brushwork are also essential skills, and when these two are used in a controlled way, they lead to many advanced techniques, such as toning and broken brushstrokes.

After the initial hard work and practice, we shall come down to the business of painting animals. The chapter about painting animals has been organized according to various styles. I have chosen the more popular and practical styles for your learning process, starting with simple sketches using an informal application of colours. It is important to be accurate with shapes and proportions in animal painting. The sketches have been designed to help you work on this aspect and they will hopefully prepare you for learning the other styles that lie ahead. Following on will be styles using the techniques of basic brushstrokes, toning and broken brushstrokes – in this order. Each succeeding style is more advanced than the one before and along with each there are illustrations suited to that technique. I may therefore repeat an animal, illustrating it in more than one style. My purpose here is to show you that each animal can be painted in many different ways. Overall, I aim to use the minimum number of brushstrokes needed to bring out the true sense – the shape, the character and the movement – of an animal. It is a challenge, but this is the beautiful essence of non-outline Chinese brush painting. The chapter concludes with a session on painting animals with patterns, allowing you freely to apply all or any of the styles you have acquired.

Some of the instructions in this book may appear to be overly technical. However, bear in mind that techniques developed by accomplished masters can be complicated. In order to make sure that you understand how to achieve them, it's necessary to lay down systematic and detailed instructions for each technique, at the same time showing you how the brush works and how your hand works. You can then refer to these instructions any time you feel the need.

In working through this book, you will find it a bonus if you have experience in painting other types of subject because you will be able to apply your basic techniques more fluently. However, I have no doubt that beginners will eventually catch up if they practise the skills and techniques, as suggested in this book. If, on the other hand, you are an artist who has already started to paint animals, this book has been designed to help you by explaining the various approaches in a systematic way. You can paint a single animal in many different ways, so there are always new avenues for advanced Chinese brush painters to consider. Hopefully, this book will provide stepping stones that will help you to understand which skills you have already mastered and discover what else is available so that you can explore further.

The Gallery section contains an exhibition of animal painting, combined with flower and landscape painting techniques. You will see how other subjects can enhance artworks in animal painting. All the artworks in this chapter are the result of simple and at times almost abstract brushstrokes, through which I hope to give you further insight into the expressive world of the Chinese brush. The only way to reach the stage at which you will be able to create similar works with your own unique insights and style is to be fluent in using the basic techniques. So it is time to make a start with the basics, repeatedly practising the many approaches and experimenting with ideas and techniques.

Animal painting requires you to be adventurous, to be inventive, to be daring and not to be afraid to experiment. Use your brush freely. Always aim to expand what you can achieve. Stretch the brush to attempt what you think is impossible. I hope I have given you a good beginning. It will be your turn to work on what you have taken here and go on expanding it. I hope that you will try painting animals other than those illustrated in this book, using the techniques you learn from here. Some day, I also hope that you will develop your own style of animal painting.

Painting animals with Chinese brushes can become a virtually endless voyage of discovery and experiment. For example, one could easily write a book about each animal that is illustrated here. It is a challenge to us that we should not stop here, but instead go forward to bring this art form to a higher level.

A BABY ELEPHANT
An elephant is a complicated animal to paint. Full instructions are given on pages 120–125.

1 MATERIALS AND EQUIPMENT

CHINESE BRUSHES

A traditional Chinese brush has a bamboo handle and a tip made of animal hair. Carved wood, animal horns and bones, ceramic, cloisonné and even jade are also used for making handles, and recently an increasing number of manufacturers have been replacing bamboo handles with wood or plastic.

Usually brushes are classified as 'soft-hair' (軟毫) or 'tough-hair' (硬毫) according to the type of hair used for making the brush tips. The soft-hairs are usually white and the tough-hairs are dyed brown or black. In animal painting, brushes used for creating hair and fur are used in a very rough way. We need tough brushes to withstand the rough treatment. We also need brushes for general painting: applying colours, creating tones and adding accompaniments, such as trees, rocks, flowers and sky. However, rough painting wears out brushes faster than usual. For this reason, it is not advisable to use the same brush for creating animal hairs and for general painting. I usually keep a few brushes exclusively for rough painting and separate them from the rest of my brushes. When those used for rough painting are worn out, replace them with those from the general painting group and buy new ones to replace those used for general painting.

SOFT-HAIR BRUSHES

The soft hairs are those of goats, chickens or lambs. Goat hair is the finest of all soft hairs and is hence the most popular for making brushes. White-hair brushes are very soft and can take in a lot of moisture. For non-outline painting, however, I prefer the flexibility of the brown-hair and black-hair brushes. I have used the white-hair brushes only for creating washes in this book. The following two types are good for this purpose.

A **Goat-hair Ti brush** (羊毫提筆) is a big brush. Ti brushes can be made of any type of hair. Soft-hair Ti brushes are good for creating washes. They can also be used for general painting, if you choose. There is a wide range of Goat-hair Ti brushes and they are generally not very expensive, so get the biggest one you can afford.

A **Hake brush** (底紋筆) is a wide, flat brush. The hair may be black or white. The white ones are made of goat hair and are cheaper than the black ones. There are five widths available in the white-hair type: 2.5 cm (1 in), 3.8 cm (1½ in), 5 cm (2 in), 6.4 cm (2½ in) and 7.6 cm (3 in).

A white soft-hair brush

A black tough-hair brush

A brown tough-hair brush

Hake brushes wider than 7.6 cm (3 in) are usually made for mounting in the traditional way. For creating washes, a brush between 5 and 7.6 cm (2 and 3 in) wide would be adequate. I keep both a 5 cm (2 in) and a 7.6 cm (3 in) hake brush. It is more convenient to have two Hake brushes when you are doing a multi-colour wash, using one brush to hold one colour and the other to hold the second colour. The 5 cm (2 in) Hake brush can also be useful for general painting. Avoid Hake brushes with metal necks because they will rust after getting wet a few times.

There is an alternative to the Hake brush, called a **Pai brush** (排筆). 'Pai' means lining up side by side. Pai brushes are made up of from two to six single brushes, linked together side by side. They usually have goat-hair brush tips. These are cheaper, but are not as well made as the Hake brushes.

TOUGH-HAIR BRUSHES

BROWN-HAIR BRUSHES

The brown tough-hair brushes are those of foxes, wolves, rabbits, camels and many other animals. Chinese brush manufacturers are continually experimenting with new brown hairs and today we have a much greater variety of brown-hair brushes than our ancient masters. Brown-hair brushes are more flexible than the soft-hair type. When the brush tip of a good-quality brown-hair brush is pressed, it fans out easily, creating broad brushstrokes. When the brush is lifted, it always returns to the upright pointed position. Different degrees of pressure on the brush tip are used to make the brush fan out to different widths. This quality makes these brushes preferable for general painting. There is a wider range of brown-hair brushes available than of those made with white or black hair. The following four differently sized brushes are my basic choice for general painting. These will enable you to create a wide range of brushstrokes.

Small Orchid and Bamboo brush (小蘭竹). This is the largest of the four. As the name suggests, it is made especially for painting bamboos and orchids. It is a popular brush for painting flowers, but we can use it for large brushwork in animal painting as well as in general painting. It is especially useful for applying colours over a large area. The Orchid and Bamboo brush is a very popular brush, so every manufacturer makes its own brand, resulting in a wide range of qualities, which makes choosing a good one very confusing. The only advice I can give you is that if you are not happy with the one you have chosen, buy one made by a different manufacturer when yours has worn out.

No.3 Leopard and Wolf brush (三号豹狼毫). This is one of the best medium-sized brushes due to the quality of hair used to make the brush tip, which is smaller and shorter than that of the Small Orchid and Bamboo brush. It is a delightful brush for painting medium-sized brushstrokes. There are usually three sizes of Leopard and Wolf brushes available: No.1, No.2 and No.3 (the smallest size). You may also find an extra-large No.1, extra-large No.2 and extra-large No.3, but only in quality art shops.

Red Bean brush (紅豆). The hairs of this brush are trimmed to form a slender point at the brush tip, making this a very useful brush for sketching and painting small-scale brushwork. The tip is dyed black and red. In ancient times, Red Bean brushes were dyed in red bean juice, hence the name.

No.1 Wolf-hair brush for Painting (一号狼毫國畫筆). This brush has a very thin brush tip, which is carefully trimmed. It is useful for final touches, such as the iris of an animal's eye or its teeth, but because it can hold only a small amount of moisture, it is not advisable to use this brush for sketching. There are many versions of these tiny brushes. The one I have chosen has the tip tugged through two tiny wooden rings. This gives extra security, keeping the little bundle of hairs in place. When you search for this brush, look out for those with the wooden rings.

A popular technique for creating animal hairs in painting is to use broken brushstrokes. To create a broken brushstroke, the brush tip of a dry brush is pressed before or after the loading of colours until the hairs separate. Either way, this is very damaging to the brush

A LIST OF ESSENTIAL BRUSHES

Below is a list of all the brushes I recommend for learning to paint animals, as described in this book.

1. No.1 Wolf-hair brush for Painting
2. Red Bean brush
3. No.3 Leopard and Wolf brush
4. Small Landscape brush
5. Large Landscape brush
6. Small Orchid and Bamboo brush
7. Goat-hair Hake brush, at least 5 cm (2 in) wide
8. Goat-hair Ti brush
9. Small Mountain and Horse brush

Optional (shown on page 19)
• Extra-large Mountain and Horse brush *or*
• Large Bear-hair brush *or*
• Wolf-hair Dou brush

1. No.1 Wolf-hair brush for Painting
2. Red Bean
3. No.3 Leopard and Wolf brush
4. Small Landscape brush
5. Large Landscape brush

hairs, and even a tough black-hair brush will wear out faster than usual. So we are looking for tough brushes in the brown-hair and black-hair categories. In general painting, we can create different sizes of brushwork by varying the angle at which the brush tip touches the paper. However, in creating broken brushwork, the brush is always held vertically, which means that you can only paint different sizes of broken brushwork by using different sizes of brush. You will therefore need more than one brush for broken brushwork. I would suggest that you have two brushes of different sizes from the brown-hair range and one from the black-hair range. For the paintings in this book, I used two landscape brushes from the brown-hair brushes and a small Mountain and Horse brush from the black-hair brushes.

Landscape brushes (山水筆). These are especially made for rough brushwork. There are three sizes of this type of brush: large, medium and small, all of which are reasonably inexpensive. A small Landscape brush and a large Landscape brush will be useful to start with. These two brushes will be used to paint small and medium broken brushwork. You will need a larger brush to paint larger broken brushwork. For this purpose, I choose a

6. Small Orchid and Bamboo brush

7. Goat-hair Hake brush, at least 5 cm (2 in) wide

8. Goat-hair Ti brush

9. Small Mountain and Horse brush

black-hair brush – the small-sized Mountain and Horse brush. We shall discuss this in detail when we come to the black-hair section. You could choose two extra-small Mountain and Horse brushes instead of the landscape brushes, but the former can be very expensive. Landscape brushes are much cheaper and this makes frequent replacement more affordable.

We also need a brush to paint the delicate features of animals, such as the nose, eyes and mouth. The No.1 Wolf-hair brush for Painting can do the job, but the tip of this brush is very small, so the brush can only hold a very small amount of ink, which means that you have constantly to keep dipping into your colour to refill, even when you are only painting an eye. Ideally, therefore, you need a very slender brush that can create thin lines and small, delicate brushwork. At the same time, it needs to carry more colour so that it can go a longer way. For this purpose, I recommend that you select an Outline brush, as I have described below.

Outline brush (勾綠筆). There are many brushes used for outline painting. This particular example is one of the most popular. If you cannot find the one I suggest here, choose one which has a very slender brush tip but is at least double the length as well as the width of the No.1 Wolf-hair brush for Painting. You most probably will find one from the range of brushes for outline painting.

BLACK-HAIR BRUSHES

The black-hair brushes are made of even firmer hair than the brown-hair type. The hairs are those of the horse, hog, raccoon and other animals with tougher hairs. These brushes carry even less moisture than the brown-hair ones. Experienced artists make use of this quality to create expressive rough and dry brushwork in landscape painting and animal painting. Brushes in this category are more expensive because hairs for making brushes of this type have to be of very high quality; if they are too old or hard, the brush will not hold moisture. They cannot be too soft either, or they will not create the special dry and rough effects.

A very popular black-hair brush is the **Mountain and Horse brush** (山馬筆). The best Mountain and Horse brushes are those that are made entirely from horsehair and are dyed black. Cheaper versions of this brush are made either with a mixture of brown hair and black hair or of brown hair that has been dyed black. I personally prefer those that are made entirely of horsehair. There are six sizes of these horsehair brushes available: large, medium, small, extra-small size 1, extra-small size 2 and extra-small size 3. For the exercises in this book, you will only require the small size. Again, let me remind you that we use brushes very roughly in animal painting. Even the hardy black-hair brushes tend to wear out faster than usual.

LARGE BRUSHES

The illustrations seen here have been scaled down for this book. Many Chinese artists paint animals in very large sizes. The bigger they are, the more expressive the brushwork, but of course you require very large brushes. I am going to recommend a few of these to you in case you would like to try painting larger artworks.

In practice, I have used two large brushes for certain of the illustrations and I will explain how they are used. However, I have also provided you with alternative instructions in case you do not wish to purchase these brushes.

Extra-large Mountain and Horse brush (特 大 山 馬 筆). There are actually three sizes in this group, but some manufacturers make only one size, which they simply call Extra-large Mountain and Horse brush. Unfortunately, the quality of Extra-large Mountain and Horse brushes varies a lot, depending on the manufacturer. Since this brush is usually very expensive, it would therefore be safer to acquire it through a reputable Chinese art material supplier.

Bear-hair brush (熊 毫 書 畫). This is a relatively new brush. Bear hair is tougher than wolf hair, but softer than horsehair. Manufacturers usually dye the hairs black and include them in the black-hair category. There are a few versions of the Bear-hair brush now available. The one I have chosen is indicated by its Chinese name above. This particular brush comes in three sizes and I have used the large size for painting some of the illustrations in this book. One warning about this brush: it can soak up a lot of moisture, so before you use it be sure to prepare a larger quantity than usual of ink or colours. Also, if the brush is wet, try to squeeze out as much moisture as possible before loading it with colour, or the extra moisture in the brush will dilute the colour and soften your intended tone.

Wolf-hair Dou brush (狼 毫 斗 筆). Dou brushes are similar to Ti brushes. Dou brushes can vary, both in the size of the brush itself and in the length of the brush tip. There are many types of Wolf-hair Dou brushes. Look for one which has a long brush tip. Get a large one that suits your pocket.

A Large Bear-hair brush.

A Wolf-hair Dou brush.

An Extra-large Mountain and Horse brush.

'OPENING' A CHINESE BRUSH

The tip of a new Chinese brush is held together neatly with gum. This is only for the purpose of presentation. The tip is also usually protected with a bamboo or plastic cover when it is new. Before using a Chinese brush for painting, the brush needs to be 'opened'. 'Opening' a brush means removing the gum and loosening the hair. Begin this process by soaking the brush tip in cold water. Avoid using hot or warm water – people sometimes use warm water to hasten the process of removing gum, but in my opinion this does not save time. Treat your brushes gently and with respect, giving them enough time to be properly opened. Using warm or hot water for the opening process generally has two effects on a brush: the hot water shrinks the hair, making it tougher and losing the shape it was trimmed into; in addition, the brush tip is secured in the handle with a little bit of glue and warm or hot water will loosen this, causing the tip to fall prematurely. Prolonged and unnecessary soaking of the brush in water will also do this, which is why you should never soak brushes in water when not in use.

Soak your new brush in a jar with sufficient cold and clean water to cover the brush tip. For the majority of brushes, twenty minutes will be sufficient to loosen the gum and the brush tips. A Ti brush or Dou brush needs a longer time for the soaking – about half an hour. After soaking the new brush in water for twenty minutes or so, press the brush tip gently with your fingers. If the hairs are soft and separate, the brush is properly 'opened'. If the tip is still hard and will not separate, do not force it by bending. Return it to the water and soak for a longer time. When the brush is fully opened, rinse it thoroughly in clean water to remove all the gum. Dry it between tissues or with a soft towel. The brush is now ready to serve you.

A fully 'opened' brush.

A new brush before being 'opened'.

CARING FOR CHINESE BRUSHES

There are a few things you can do to keep your brushes in good condition and help them to last longer.

Do not put your opened brush back into its bamboo or plastic cover. When a brush is opened, the brush tip will be too big for the cover and squeezing it back in will damage or distort the hairs.

Do not store wet or damp brushes in airtight containers, such as plastic bags. Chinese brushes are made of natural materials and they can rot in damp conditions. Always dry them completely before storing them away. When the brushes are not in use, you can store them in opened jars, with the tips of the brushes pointing up. Brushes that come with loops of cord at the top can be hung on specially made brush hangers. You will find these hangers for sale in the shops where you get your Chinese brushes. It's also easy to make one.

If you need to carry the brushes with you on painting trips or to and from classes, the best way is to wrap them in specially made brush mats. These are made up of thin bamboo sticks bound together and have gaps to allow brushes to breathe and dry. Unfortunately, if you are not careful, your precious brushes will fall out from the open ends and get lost. However, I have a trick for keeping the brushes securely in place within the mat: cut a length of dressmaking elastic, equal to the width of the mat, and thread it through the gaps of the mat, securing the two ends of the elastic with stitches. The loops formed by the elastic are perfect for holding the brushes.

CHINESE BRUSH MAT
I have threaded dressmaking elastic through this bamboo mat and secured the elastic at both ends with stitches.

Do not use a quality brush for mixing colours. Either get a cheap watercolour brush for this purpose or use an old Chinese brush.

After each painting session, always clean your brushes and rid them of as much ink and colour as possible. Sometimes you will find that it is difficult to get rid of colours and ink stuck around the neck of the brush. When this happens, soak the brush in a jar of clean water and let the colours diffuse into the water. This will help to remove most of the colour, though perhaps not all. Wipe off excess moisture before storing brushes away. Do not clean any of your brushes with soap or washing-up liquid. Washing-up liquid and soap, once attached to the hair, are difficult to get rid of and can sometimes form a barrier, causing you problems when picking up colours with the brush.

The brush tip of a quality brown-hair or black-hair brush always returns to a point when wet. When this fails to happen, the brush has passed its serving time and you should consider replacing it with a new one. However, do not discard the old brushes, as they can be used for mixing colours. The big ones are also perfect for rough and dry brushwork, as used to suggest fur.

PAPER

We use **Xuan paper** (宣紙) for Chinese animal painting. This paper is made from a mixture of tree barks, plants, bamboo, cotton and other materials. The proportions of each material differ from manufacturer to manufacturer and each manufacturer guards their secret formula for making their brand of Xuan paper. Some of these formulae have been passed on from ancient times and each one has a name. This is usually printed at one corner of a sheet or across the side of a pack of 50 or 100 sheets. Xuan papers are usually available in loose sheets measuring approximately 66 x 132 cm (26 x 52 in), though some varieties are bigger. There are two types of Xuan paper: the absorbent unsized Xuan and the alum-sized Xuan. In non-outline animal painting, we use the absorbent type.

Chinese absorbent Xuan paper is available in different thickness. We call the thinnest 'one-sheet' (單宣); the next thickness is 'two-sheet' (二層夾宣) or (雙夾宣); then comes 'three-sheet' (三層夾宣) or (三夾宣), while the thickest is 'four-sheet' (四層夾宣) or (四夾宣).

The 'one-sheet' papers are relatively cheaper than the others, so it is economical to use these for learning and for practice. The 'two-sheet' ones are more suitable for serious painting. Chinese artists prefer the 'three-sheet' and 'four-sheet' Xuan paper for animal painting, but these papers are seldom available outside China. Even in Asia, only shops specializing in quality Chinese painting materials stock the 'three-sheet' and 'four-sheet' papers. In many cases, 'four-sheet' Xuan papers seldom make the trip from the factory to

1. Absorbent 'one-sheet' Xuan paper.

2. Absorbent 'two-sheet' Xuan paper.

3. Absorbent 'three-sheet' Xuan paper.

4. Absorbent 'four-sheet' Xuan paper.

the shop because artists sweep them all up as soon as they are made. In places where 'four-sheet' absorbent Xuan paper is not available, some artists will go as far as to paste two 'two-sheet' papers together to create a 'four-sheet' one. The Xuan paper that is available in the UK is usually of the one-sheet thickness, but art shops that stock Chinese painting materials can always order the 'two-sheet' thickness for you if you want a sufficiently large quantity. Absorbent Xuan paper is usually sold as loose sheets or large packs. Sometimes the papers can be cut in half lengthwise and sold as rolls of 12 or 15 half-sheets.

Besides the Chinese, the Japanese and the Koreans also make Xuan Paper. There is one made according to a Japanese formula called '**Moon Palace**' (月宮殿). This Xuan paper is of 'two-sheet' thickness in continuous rolls, usually of about 15 metres (50 feet) long for each roll. There are three widths available: 38 cm (15 in) wide, 45.5 cm (18 in) wide and 61 cm (24 in) wide. The advantage of this paper is that it is widely available in art shops. It has a smooth side and a rough side. I usually advise my pupils to use the smooth side for painting, though some artists prefer the rough side for painting rough and dry brushwork. Moon Palace is a good-quality Xuan paper. If you are happy and comfortable with it, I do not see any reason why you cannot continue to use it. However, it's worth pointing out that Moon Palace is not everyone's favourite, as many people find it difficult to control the absorbency of this paper.

A roll of Moon Palace, 38 cm (15 in) wide.

You can cut a piece of absorbent Xuan paper, whether it comes in a loose sheet or in a continuous roll, with a wet brush. Draw a line with a wet brush where you want to make the cut and then pull the paper apart. The two sides of paper will separate easily.

Other beautiful absorbent Xuan papers come dyed with a variety of colours. The most popular ones for animal painting are the ones tinted with blue or green. You can also make your own tinted paper with colour washes. Instructions for applying colour washes can be found in the Appendix on page 172. You can also create paper with multi-tone or multi-colour washes. This is especially useful, as Xuan papers tinted with more than one colour or tone of a colour are seldom available in the shops.

Above: Green and blue absorbent Xuan paper.

Above: Flower Xuan paper and smooth-textured Mulberry paper.

There are other Xuan papers that have extra texture in them. For example, the speckled gold papers have bits of gold paper mixed in the pulp when the papers are made. There are red, pink, beige and white gold-speckled papers. These are popular for paintings for celebrations, such as Chinese New Year, when people like to paint the animal of that year on the red gold-speckled paper, or to celebrate a person's birthday by painting the animal of the year the person was born. There is also a paper with flowers and leaves embedded in it. This one has an atmosphere of nature and gives a very pleasant background to animal painting. However, the textured papers are not a favourite among animal artists because the bits can sometimes distract people from the delicately painted features of animals.

Mulberry paper (麻 紙) is another good-quality absorbent paper for painting. This paper is slower to absorb moisture than the usual absorbent Xuan paper, allowing the brushwork to be more controlled. The mulberry paper made for Chinese painting is not the same as that made for craftwork: the papers made for Chinese painting have a tighter texture and are available in two types. One type is coarse, with beautiful patterns created by the mulberry fibres. Washes painted on this paper have a very dramatic effect. The other type has smooth texture. Mulberry paper can be white, light beige or dark beige in colour. Animal painters prefer the smooth type because too great a density of fibres can distract the eye from the detailed features of animals, especially the facial features.

I personally prefer the three-sheet and four-sheet thickness of Xuan paper for animal artworks. However, since most readers will not be able to get hold of these, I have used loose sheets of two-sheet absorbent Xuan paper for all the illustrations in this book. If absorbent Xuan paper of one-sheet thickness is the only type available to you, it is perfectly fine to use it, but try not to load your brush with too much moisture during painting. I shall give you tips about loading the brush with ink or colours as much as possible throughout the book. It is also advisable to change your underlining sheets more often before they get too wet.

Below: White mulberry paper with texture and speckled gold paper in pale beige.

INK

Non-outline Chinese animal painting is very ink-dominated, so I shall generally be using ink in this book.

It is traditional to make ink by grinding an ink stick on an ink stone and this was the way our ancient masters made their ink. However, liquid ink has been around for quite a long time and many artists now use it for painting. There is always a difference of opinion over whether we should only use ink made by an ink stick or whether it is acceptable to use liquid ink. Many argue that ink made by grinding is thicker and of better quality, claiming that one can achieve different grades and tones only by using ink made in this way. I personally would not agree with this. After all, both ink sticks and liquid ink are made from the same ingredients. I feel it's a matter of habit and knowing how to use your ink. There are many types of good-quality liquid ink that are very thick and very dark. I am convinced that either type of ink will serve the purpose and everyone should be allowed to choose without feeling guilty about it. I shall therefore provide you with information about both types and leave you to choose which is most suitable to you and your way of working.

Ink used for animal painting has to be thick and dark and you need plenty of it. If you are using ground ink, be sure to make a large quantity of thick, dark ink. Ink dries up easily. It can be very frustrating if you have to stop halfway through painting an animal because you have run out of ink and then have to spend quite some time making a fresh batch in order to resume your painting. For convenience, therefore, I would suggest readers use liquid ink, at least for learning and practising.

USING INK STICKS

For those who would like to make ink with an ink stick, you will also need an ink stone. A traditional ink stone is made of a kind of stone similar to slate, but much harder. Modern ink stones can be made from various materials, including stone, agate, ceramic, plaster and even jade. The price of an ink stone can vary from £2 to over £20,000. Though the quality of an expensive one is always better, a cheaper one will serve the purpose equally well. There are many sizes available. Always choose one that allows the ink stick to move comfortably on it in a circular motion. Alternatively, you can use an unglazed ceramic bowl instead of an ink stone. When I enrolled as a pupil to my first master, he gave me a ceramic bowl to start with because I was not considered worthy to use an ink stone yet. I still use this bowl for grinding my ink and it has now served me for more than fifty years.

As for ink sticks, prices also vary from less than £1 to about £50. Antique ink sticks are priced at well over £1000. Ink sticks are classified by names. The name of an ink stick is usually engraved on the stick. The most basic ones available in the UK are called Qian Qiu Guang (千 秋 光) and Zi Yu Guang (紫 玉 光). These ink sticks are usable, but their qualities are not remarkable. However, they are perfectly fine for anyone who is just starting Chinese painting, as you may be.

A basic ink stick with a traditional ink stone.

Tie Zhäi Weng (鐵齋翁書畫寶墨) is an ink stick of much better quality. It is also much more expensive. Unfortunately, many imitations of this particular ink stick are offered at lower prices on the market. Also available are many other ink sticks with beautiful pictures engraved on them. These are more for presentation than an indication of quality, as they are more or less the same as the two I mentioned first.

If you want to make ink with an ink stick, this is how you make it: first place your ink stone or ceramic bowl on a level surface and then use your brush or an eyedropper to place a few drops of clean water on the surface of the ink stone. Hold the ink stone with one hand so that it will not move around when you are grinding the ink stick on it. Hold the ink stick with the other hand, placing it vertically on the water drops and grinding against the surface of the stone in circular motion. You will see dark ink starting to appear. Add a few more drops of water and grind again. Repeat the process of adding a few drops of water, followed by grinding, until you have made sufficient dark ink. It is not advisable to grind the ink stick on a large pool of water. It will take a long time to turn the large pool of water into thick ink. Besides, thick ink dries up quickly. Test the darkness of the ink from time to time to see whether it is sufficiently dark and thick for your use. Add more water if required.

When you finish grinding, do not rest the wet part of the ink stick on the ink stone or it will stick to the stone when it dries. When the ink you prepared has almost run out, repeat the grinding process again. Always clean the ink stone every time after use. Any dry leftover ink on the stone will be very difficult to remove. Clean the stone with soft tissues and cold water. Dry it properly before putting it away. Do not use any abrasive material to clean the stone. Hard and abrasive material will damage the delicate surface of the stone.

Many readers have asked me how to restore an ink stone which has hard crusts of leftover ink stuck on the surface. The following method may help you to remove most of the leftover ink, but it will not necessarily restore your stone to its original perfect beauty. Fill a large bowl with warm water. The water should not be hot, just warm enough to touch. Use an old plastic bowl because the black ink may leave stains. Soak your ink stone in it. After ten minutes, use tissues or paper towels to wipe away the top layer of ink slowly, which by now should be softened. Soak the ink stone again for ten more minutes and again wipe off the softened ink with soft papers. Repeat the process of soaking and wiping to remove as much leftover ink as possible. Wear waterproof gloves when you do this because the dark ink will stain your hands. If the water gets cold, you can pour it away and refill the bowl with clean, warm water. However, it is not essential to change the water. When you have removed as much leftover ink as you can, rinse the ink stone and wipe it with paper towels. Leave it to dry before storing it away.

USING LIQUID INK

If you are going to use liquid ink, it is more economical to buy a large bottle than a small one. There are many manufacturers of quality liquid ink in China. A reliable one is called – 得閣 , which is probably the oldest ink maker in China. They make many types of ink, liquid as well as sticks, with different qualities. The liquid ink they make for general use is shown opposite. This is the most basic type. The same manufacturer also produces better qualities of ink. Some of their finest liquid inks are stored and sealed in porcelain jars and these are fast becoming collector's items.

Ink intended for writing runs madly on absorbent paper. You cannot create dry brushwork with writing ink, so it is not suitable for Chinese brush painting. The Chinese ink has gum in it and when it is dry it is permanent on paper. For this reason you are advised not to wear your best clothing when you are using Chinese ink, as you will not be able to remove any splashes that accidentally fall on to your clothing.

It is best to pour liquid ink into a different container to the one used for mixing colours. If your mixing dish has several compartments, use one compartment exclusively for ink. You can use the traditional ink stone, a small ceramic dish or even a small plastic container. Make sure that you clean the ink dish every time you finish painting. Any leftover ink will harden and prove very difficult to remove.

When freshly poured out of the bottle, liquid ink may be a bit thin, but it will thicken up very quickly if it is left in the open air. I usually allow fresh ink to stand for five to ten minutes before using it. For the same reason, you should pour out only a small amount of ink every time and add to it when it is running out. If the ink becomes too thick, you can add a bit of fresh ink to thin it. Adding water will make it paler, so always add fresh ink for thinning purposes if you want dark ink for painting.

I have used ready-made liquid ink for all the examples and artworks in this book. The following are some terms I use:

Dark ink. This is ink that has been freshly poured out of the bottle and has not been left in the open for too long. Dark ink is suitable for general painting.

Diluted ink. Water can be added to the dark ink. The more water you add, the lighter the ink will become. Diluted ink is used for general painting and for shading. It is often used for toning.

Medium ink. A tiny bit of dark ink can be added to diluted ink to make it darker. You can create medium ink of different tones by controlling the amount of dark ink you add.

Thick ink. This is dark ink that has been left in the open for some time to thicken up. Thick ink is useful for creating dry brushwork and I use this consistency frequently in animal painting.

Liquid ink for general use

COLOURS

There are many types of colour that are suitable. The ones especially made for Chinese painting are usually manufactured in China, Japan or Korea. They come in either powder or crystal form. You have to prepare the powder colours with gum before use, whereas crystals have gum pre-mixed into them. There are also colours that come either in trays or tubes.

Some people insist on using colours manufactured in China or Japan for Chinese painting. Personally, I see no reason why English watercolours should not be used. Most of my pupils use these with excellent results, and there is the added advantage that English watercolours are widely available and there is a good range.

Because Chinese and Japanese colours have gum in them, it makes life easier if you want to mount Xuan-paper artworks in the traditional way, since you have to wet your paintings for the mounting process. English watercolours, however, tend to run when you wet paintings. Fortunately, my modern method of mounting eliminates this headache and all my pupils have used this technique successfully. I have therefore used English watercolours for the illustrations in this book, all of which are mounted this way. You will find the instruction for this method in my other books, *Chinese Calligraphy Made Easy* and *Chinese Flower Painting Made Easy*.

The following is a list of colours used in this book (you can, of course, add any of your favourites to the list):

Sap green   indigo   burnt sienna   gamboge   yellow ochre
cadmium yellow   cadmium orange   cadmium red deep
alizarin crimson   permanent rose   cobalt blue   process white

Please feel free to use any of the Chinese, Japanese or Korean colours, but remember to follow the manufacturer's instructions when using them.

Sap green

Gamboge

Burnt sienna

Indigo

OTHER ACCESSORIES

In addition to paper, brushes, ink and paint, you will need the items listed below, most of which you will already have around the house.

- A big jar or a yoghurt pot for water – if you prefer, you can have a few jars, so you don't have to keep changing to clean water.
- A mixing dish with a few compartments or, alternatively, a big light-coloured dinner plate; if you use a plate for mixing colours, you will also need to use a small container or an ink stone for your ink.
- Lots of newspaper, to protect the surface you are painting on.
- A large-sized clean (unused) sheet of newsprint (plain, inexpensive, absorbent paper) on which to lay your Xuan paper. This is needed to absorb excess moisture during painting. When the newsprint gets too wet and muddy, you can change to a fresh one. Traditionally, Chinese artists used to lay their painting paper on a large piece of flannel. Flannels produced for this purpose are available in art shops that stock Chinese painting materials. You can, however, just get a large piece of flannel from a fabric shop. Personally, I find that flannels are too soft and can be a hindrance to any expressive movement. Newsprint serves the same purpose well, but you have to change it frequently. Most art or craft shops stock newsprint, but usually in very small sizes. Look for A1 sheets. If these are not in stock, the shop can easily order them for you, and you will find it cheaper to buy in bulk. Another option, if there is a fish and chip shop near you, is to ask if they will sell you some of theirs, as most of them use newsprint to wrap their food.
- Small stones or brass weights, to keep your painting paper from moving when you are painting.
- A cheap painting brush or an old Chinese brush for mixing colours.
- A few wide, shallow containers, such as shallow bowls or small, wide yoghurt pots, for mixing washes – they should be wider than the width of your hake brush.
- Paper towels for wiping brushes dry, because you are going to be using dry brushes a lot for your animal paintings.

Cobalt blue

Permanent rose

Alizarin crimson

Cadmium red deep

2 BASIC TECHNIQUES

Non-outline animal painting using the Chinese brush is a very expressive art form. If you are a beginner, you may find that your hands are reluctant, hesitant, and not moving as you wish. Don't worry: everybody starts off like this. Constant practice with the brush will soon improve your skills. The important thing is to understand your brush, getting to know how it works. Combine this with plenty of practice, and your confidence will soon grow.

I am going to cover all the basic techniques in this chapter in a simple way, without going into details about the different applications. When we come to paint the animals in the next chapter, I shall show you all the variations you'll need. You will then be using the basic techniques explained here and combining brushstrokes as well as expanding them to develop further techniques to suit each animal we are going to paint.

MANOEUVRING CHINESE BRUSHES

If you do not have much experience in using a Chinese brush, this is where you start. Your first step is to learn how to hold the brush in the correct way. Then you will learn how to use it effectively. Simple details, such as the angle of the brush to the painting surface and the direction in which you move the brush, all contribute to the final outcome. It may be confusing to learn so many things at the beginning, but don't give up. Constant practice with your brush will soon improve your skills.

ANATOMY OF A CHINESE BRUSH

Handle

Neck

Brush tip

Nib

HOLDING THE BRUSH

The length of the handle of a Chinese brush is carefully measured in proportion to the size of the brush tip and with regard to the way the brush is intended to be used. For example, a brush made with black hair has a longer handle in comparison to a brush that is of the same size, but made with a different type of hair. The reason for this is that a black-hair brush is made for expressive painting. It therefore needs a longer handle, so that you can swing the brush during painting to achieve sweeping brushstrokes.

The normal way to hold a brush is to hold it at the centre of the handle. Experienced artists sometimes vary the position for special effects. For newcomers to the Chinese brush, it is better to start with the middle position. When you are more comfortable with the brush, you can then experiment with different positions.

When you hold the brush at the middle of the handle, your arm will always be positioned away from the painting surface. This gives you freedom to move your hand and arm in any direction without being restricted. Freedom of movement is essential for expressive painting. However, when you are using a slender brush to paint detailed features, such as the eyes, nose and mouth of an animal, you may need some support to keep your hand steady. I shall show you a way to deal with this later (see page 45).

The simplest way to hold a brush is between your thumb and your four fingers. Another way is to hold it with two fingers on one side of the brush and the other two fingers on the same side as the thumb. You can use whichever way makes you feel most comfortable, as both enable you to hold the brush upright and firmly. Hold your brush in an upright position, varying the angle of the brush to the paper by rotating your wrist. Hold your brush firmly when you paint; this way you will produce brushwork with strength.

Hold the brush at the centre of the handle.

Hold the brush firmly and in an upright position.

One way of holding the brush is with four fingers on one side of the brush and the thumb on the other side.

Another way is to hold the brush with two fingers on one side and two fingers on the same side as the thumb.

ANGLE OF THE BRUSH TO THE PAINTING SURFACE

You can hold your brush either in a vertical position or at an angle to the painting surface, rotating your wrist to vary the angle of the brush to the paper. The angle often affects the outcome of the brushwork. For example, if you hold a brush loaded with ink at a high angle and touch the paper, the mark it makes is small because the contact area between the brush and paper is small. The brush mark will be larger if you hold the brush at a low angle because the contact area between the brush and the paper is proportionally larger.

Remember always to adjust the angle by rotating the wrist: do not use your fingers to adjust the angle because you will end up in holding the brush loosely, which results in loose, floppy work.

Brush held at a high angle to the paper

A small brush mark
Dip the No.3 Leopard and Wolf brush into ink. Hold it at a high angle and touch the paper.

Brush held at a low angle

A larger brush mark
Dip your No.3 Leopard and Wolf brush into the ink. Hold it at a low angle and touch the paper.

DIRECTION OF THE TIP OF THE BRUSH

The rotation of the wrist not only controls the angle of the brush to the painting surface but it also controls the direction in which the tip of the brush points. This page illustrates the most common directions. For each direction, I have demonstrated how both a right-handed and a left-handed person should hold the brush. As I am right-handed, the other illustrations in this book will simply show the right-handed position, so left-handed readers will need to adjust accordingly.

The position of the tip of a brush controls the shape of many brushstrokes. For example, if you hold your brush loaded with ink at an angle to the paper, with the tip of the brush pointing to the left, and then press the brush on the paper, the resulting brush mark will have a narrow end pointing to the left. The narrow end of the brush mark will point to the right if you point the tip of the brush to the right when you paint. It is important to know the shapes of your brushstrokes in animal painting because these shapes make up the contour of the body of the animal.

Holding the brush with the tip of the brush pointing to the right (for right-handed readers) and the handle pointing to the left.

Holding the brush with the tip of the brush pointing to the right (for left-handed readers).

A brush mark with the narrow end pointing to the right.

Holding the brush with the tip of the brush pointing to the left (for right-handed readers) and the handle pointing to the right.

Holding the brush with the tip of the brush pointing to the left (for left-handed readers).

A brush mark with the narrow end pointing to the left.

Holding the brush with the tip of the brush pointing away from you (for right-handed readers) and the handle towards you.

A brush mark with the narrow end pointing away from you.

Holding the brush with the tip of the brush pointing away from you (for left-handed readers).

Holding the brush with the tip of the brush pointing towards you (for right-handed readers) and the handle pointing away from you.

A brush mark with the narrow end pointing towards you.

Holding the brush with the tip of the brush pointing towards you (for left-handed readers).

DIRECTION OF THE HANDLE OF THE BRUSH

Some brushstrokes in animal painting need to convey a sense of swift movement and must be painted rapidly. It is more natural, and actually easier, to move the brush in the direction in which the handle is pointing when you want to paint this sort of brushstroke. As an example, consider painting the tail of a running horse, flowing to the right. Hold the brush at an angle to the paper so that the handle is pointing to the right, then paint the tail by moving the brush quickly from left to right, in the direction in which the handle is pointing. You can see that the resulting brushstroke is smooth and flowing. However, if you want to paint the tail flowing towards the left, but you are still holding the brush with the handle pointing to the right, and you move the brush in the opposite direction, that is from right to left, your movement will go against the loose hair at the tip of the brush, and the resulting brushwork will appear hesitant. This will spoil the flowing effect of the brushstroke. Some artists make use of the effect created by moving against the loose hair of the brush, but I shall not be using this effect in this book.

Sometimes, you have to change direction during a long brushstroke. For example, when you are painting a snake, you have to change direction a few times to show the coil of the body. To make this kind of brushwork effectively, always rotate your wrist to adjust the direction of the handle of the brush so it points in the direction of the painting movement.

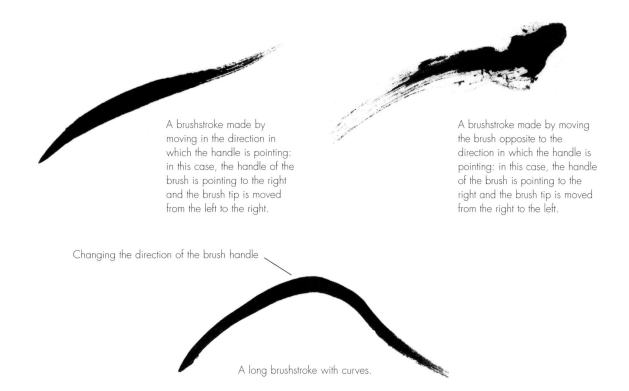

A brushstroke made by moving in the direction in which the handle is pointing: in this case, the handle of the brush is pointing to the right and the brush tip is moved from the left to the right.

A brushstroke made by moving the brush opposite to the direction in which the handle is pointing: in this case, the handle of the brush is pointing to the right and the brush tip is moved from the right to the left.

Changing the direction of the brush handle

A long brushstroke with curves.

LOADING A BRUSH WITH INK OR COLOURS

You load a brush with ink or colours to paint. Below are some of the terms I use in this book to refer to loading a brush.

Fully Loading a Brush

Dip the whole tip of a brush into ink or a colour until it is saturated. If there is too little colour in the palette, or if this is too shallow or the brush too large, hold the brush so that it is laid on its side. Roll the tip of the brush until it is saturated with colour. Next, hold the brush at an angle to the paper and touch the paper. The paper will absorb the moisture and the brush mark usually runs.

If you fully load a large brush, such as the large Bear-hair brush, you have to prepare much more colour than usual because a large brush will soak up a lot of moisture. If a large brush is not fully loaded, the brushstrokes it makes will have blank spaces.

An ink brush mark using a fully loaded Small Orchid and Bamboo brush, held at an angle to the paper.

An ink brush mark using a fully loaded large Bear-hair brush, held at an angle to the paper.

Dipping the Nib in Colour or in Ink

Here, you load only the nib of the brush with ink or colour. This will limit the amount of moisture held by the brush, so the resulting mark will be smaller.

Throughout the book, I have used the Red Bean brush and diluted ink to draw the initial outlines of animals. I wanted the initial outlines to be thin, so I dipped only the nib of the brush into diluted ink. Overloading the Red Bean brush with diluted ink will simply make your outlines thicker.

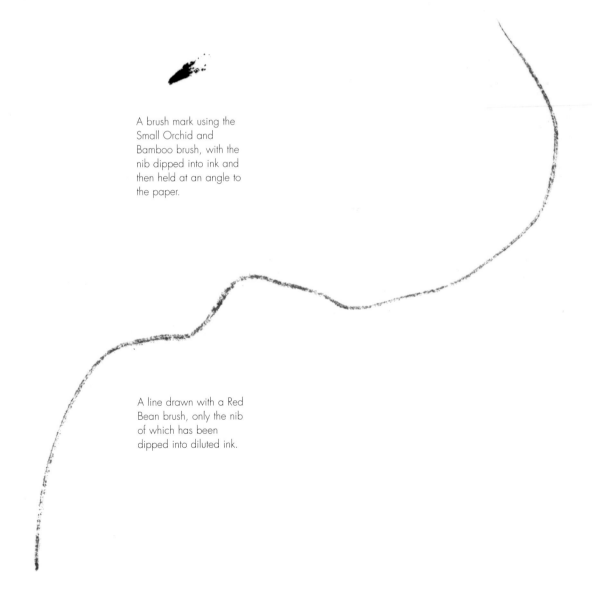

A brush mark using the Small Orchid and Bamboo brush, with the nib dipped into ink and then held at an angle to the paper.

A line drawn with a Red Bean brush, only the nib of which has been dipped into diluted ink.

Normal Loading

The normal way of loading a brush for general painting is to load a brush fully with a colour and then gently wipe off excess moisture at the edge of the colour dish. I generally use normal loading when I apply colour to paint the bodies of animals. A tip for colouring animals: you have to keep moving the brush at a steady speed. Never let the brush stay on one spot for too long or the paper will absorb the moisture from the brush. This will create unwanted bleeding of colours beyond your intended outline.

When you are using the Outline brush for drawing the delicate features of the animals, such as the faces and feet, do not load just the nib of the brush, but use normal loading. The Outline brush is designed to create thin lines, even with normal loading. If you load only the nib of an Outline brush with ink or colour, it will not last very long and you will have to keep loading it again and again in order to finish the drawing. Also, in order to create more striking and delicate features, such as the face, with the Outline brush, use thicker ink. After pouring it out of the bottle, leave the ink in the open for about five to ten minutes to thicken before you use it.

A brush mark painted using normal loading
Fully load the Small Orchid and Bamboo brush with ink and wipe off excess moisture at the side of the palette. Hold the brush at a high angle to the paper, and then press and draw a line.

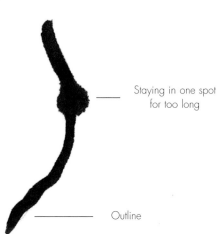

Staying in one spot for too long

Outline

Bleeding beyond the outline
This is what happens if you let the brush stay in one spot so the paper soaks up the moisture. Notice how the colour bleeds beyond the outline.

Drawing with the Outline brush with normal loading and thick ink.

Dry Loading

For drier brushwork, load a brush with a colour and wipe off excess moisture on a tissue or paper towel. The more moisture you wipe off, the drier the resulting brushwork.

A drier brush mark
Load the Small Orchid and Bamboo brush with dry loading. Holding the brush at an angle to the paper, press and paint a brushstroke.

Broken Brushstrokes

Before or after dry loading the brush with colour, press it on the palette until the hairs separate and then paint a brushstroke. The brushstroke will have lines, with blank spaces in between. We call this brushstroke a broken brushstroke. If you load the brush with colour before pressing, make sure you press the brush on the palette. Do not press the brush on a paper towel or any absorbent surface because this will absorb most of the moisture, leaving less than you intended in the brush. In order to make the broken brushstrokes more effective, use thicker ink and colour.

We frequently use broken brushstrokes when creating animal hair and fur. I shall deal with this special technique in greater detail on pages 128–133.

A broken brushstroke made with the small Mountain and Horse brush, using ink.

Two-Tone Loading or Two-Colour Loading

Two-tone and two-colour loading are popular techniques in animal painting. The nib of the brush controls the arrangement of colours. The darker colour or tone is usually loaded only on to the nib of the brush. It is important to position the nib of the brush in the right place in your painting so that the eventual brushwork will have the correct colours in the planned arrangement.

Two-tone loading

Fully load a Small Orchid and Bamboo brush with diluted burnt sienna and then dip the nib of the brush into burnt sienna. Hold the brush at a low angle, with the nib of the brush pointing to the left, and then press. The resulting brush mark will show a gradual toning of the colour. Note that the darker tone of burnt sienna is at the point where the nib touches the paper.

Two-colour loading

Fully load the Small Orchid and Bamboo brush with burnt sienna and then dip the nib of the brush into ink. Hold the brush at an angle, with the nib of the brush pointing to the left. Press and paint a line. Move the brush from left to right. The line will begin with the colour at the nib (the ink), gradually changing to the first colour loaded onto the brush (burnt sienna).

PAINTING FEATURES

When you use the Outline brush to paint features, such as the eyes, nose or mouth of an animal, the lines have to be thin and accurate. You need a steady hand for this, which is difficult if you have not been using a Chinese brush for very long. The following two methods will help.

Method 1

Hold your brush at a lower position along the handle so that your wrist touches the paper. This gives you extra support for your hand. Be aware, however, that if you are not careful, your wrist may accidentally touch the wet colour during the painting process and mess up your brushwork.

Painting surface

Method 1

Method 2: The Cushion Method

This method of holding the brush is the one I prefer. Hold the brush in the usual way, at the middle of the handle. Lay the arm of the hand which you are not using to hold the brush on the painting surface, next to the area where you are going to paint. Then rest the arm of your brush-holding hand on top of the wrist of the hand that is lying on the paper. This will give you extra support while allowing you freedom to move because you can slide your arm along the hand that is lying on the surface. I prefer this method because your hand will not interfere with your brushwork.

This technique has been used for a long time. I cannot recall any master giving it a name, however, so I am calling it the cushion method, which will make it easy to refer to later on in the book.

Method 2

WRIST AND ELBOW MOVEMENT

The Chinese non-outline style is a very expressive way in which to paint animals. It requires our hands and arms to move without hesitation. These fluid movements create the dynamic atmosphere of the final artwork. Not many people are used to moving their hands and arms actively when painting, so at first you may find your joints are very stiff and reluctant. In order to get you into the habit of moving freely and actively, let's start with two movements: the wrist movement and the elbow movement.

WRIST MOVEMENT

The wrist movement is made by rotating the wrist. We have discussed how, by rotating the wrist, we can vary the angle between the brush and the paper and also control the painting movement by positioning the direction in which the handle of the brush points. In this section, we are going to learn how to move the brush by rotating the wrist. The movements made by rotating the wrist are small, so brushstrokes made with wrist movements are restricted. They are useful for the more precise and smaller strokes, such as those needed for the features of an animal's face and its paws.

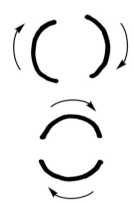

WRIST MOVEMENT
You can move your hand up or down and to the right or left by rotating the wrist.

Short vertical lines
Load the No.3 Leopard and Wolf brush with a normal loading of ink. Holding the brush in the vertical position, draw short vertical lines. Move your hand upwards and downwards with the wrist, following the directions indicated by the arrows.

Short horizontal lines
Load the No.3 Leopard and Wolf brush with a normal loading of ink. Hold the brush in a vertical position and draw short horizontal lines. Move the hand to the right or to the left with the wrist, following the directions indicated by the arrows.

Small curves
Load the No.3 Leopard and Wolf brush with a normal loading of ink. Hold the brush in a vertical position and draw the small curves. Move the brush, following the directions indicated by the arrows shown above.

ELBOW MOVEMENT

You can move your whole arm at the elbow. In this way, you can move your arm forwards or backwards and you can also swing it to the left or right. Elbow movements enable you to create longer brushstrokes. When the elbow movement is used with speed, the resulting brushwork is very dynamic. We always use dynamic and sweeping brushwork of this type to express the movements of animals.

ELBOW MOVEMENT
Move your arm forwards or backwards and to the left or right.

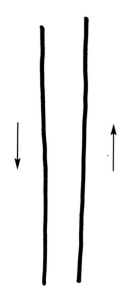

Long horizontal lines
Load the No.3 Leopard and Wolf brush with a normal loading of ink. Hold the brush in a vertical position. Draw long horizontal lines by moving your arm to the left or right, using elbow movements and following the directions indicated by the arrows.

Long vertical lines
Load the No.3 Leopard and Wolf brush with a normal loading of ink. Hold the brush in a vertical position. Draw long vertical lines by moving your arm forwards and backwards, using elbow movements and following the directions indicated by the arrows shown above.

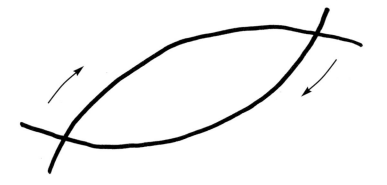

Long curves
Load the No.3 Leopard and Wolf brush with a normal loading of ink. Hold the brush in a vertical position. Draw long curves by moving your arm, as indicated in the illustrations.

EXERCISES

We generally have to use a combination of wrist and elbow movements to draw an animal. Here are some exercises to help you to practise these two movements as they are used in animal painting. I used the Red Bean brush and ink to draw the illustrations. To draw thicker lines, such as the markings on the tiger's face, use multiple thin lines to make up the thickness.

LEAPING DOLPHIN
In order to express the streamlined body of a dolphin jumping or swimming, use sweeping elbow movements to draw the lines of the body. You can then add the other details with wrist movements.

HEAD OF A TIGER
Use the cushion method to steady your hand when you draw the features of the face. Use wrist movements for shorter brushwork and elbow movement for longer strokes. To draw thicker lines, such as the markings on the face, use multiple lines to make up the thickness.

MOUSE
Use wrist movements to draw the head and elbow movements for the body and long, sweeping tail.

JUMPING HARE
Use elbow movements for the longer brushstrokes and wrist movements for details.

PRESS-AND-LIFT TECHNIQUE

When you press the brush, the hairs of the tip spread and create width in your brushwork. When you lift the brush, the tip will go back to the original pointed shape and the resulting brushwork will be thinner. By pressing and lifting the brush, you can vary the widths at different parts of a single brushstroke.

Combining the press-and-lift technique with wrist and elbow movements, you can create small and large brushstrokes of different widths and lengths. In the non-outline style of painting, an animal is made up of many brushstrokes. Each will be different in shape and size, according to how much you press or lift the brush, whether you use wrist or elbow movements, how high or low you hold the angle of the brush to the paper and how you manoeuvre the brush in changing the direction of the handle. These brushstrokes will build the shape, muscle and body as well as adding movement and giving character to the animal.

PRESS-AND-LIFT TECHNIQUE WITH WRIST MOVEMENT

PAINTING A PRESS-AND-LIFT BRUSHSTROKE WITH WRIST MOVEMENT

Unfinished brush mark

Unfinished brush mark

A brush mark made by the press-and-lift technique, with wrist movement

STEP 1
Fully load the Small Orchid and Bamboo brush with dark ink. Hold the brush at a fairly high angle to the paper. Point the handle of the brush in the direction where your movement will be going. I am positioning the handle pointing to the right in this illustration. Press at the beginning of the shape.

STEP 2
Rotate your wrist in an anti-clockwise direction so that the handle of the brush rotates, with the wrist moving the tip of the brush from left to right.

STEP 3
Lift the brush gradually as you move to the right towards the end of the shape, until it leaves the paper.

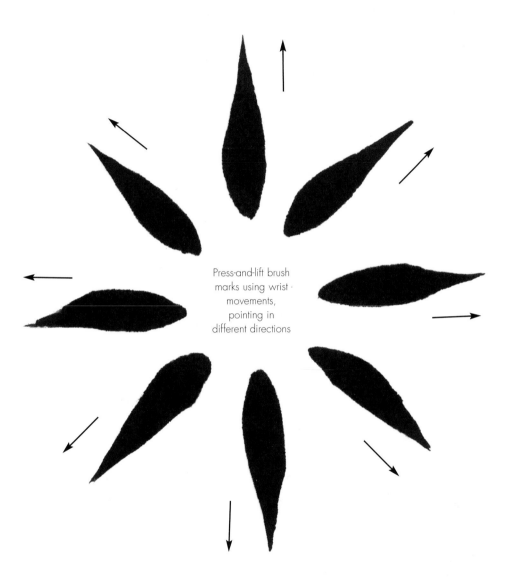

Press-and-lift brush marks using wrist movements, pointing in different directions

By adjusting the direction in which the handle of the brush points, you can angle the shape to point to different directions. The arrows indicate the direction in which the handle of the brush points at the start of each brushstroke.

PRESS-AND-LIFT TECHNIQUE WITH ELBOW MOVEMENT

**PAINTING A PRESS-AND-LIFT BRUSHSTROKE
WITH ELBOW MOVEMENT**

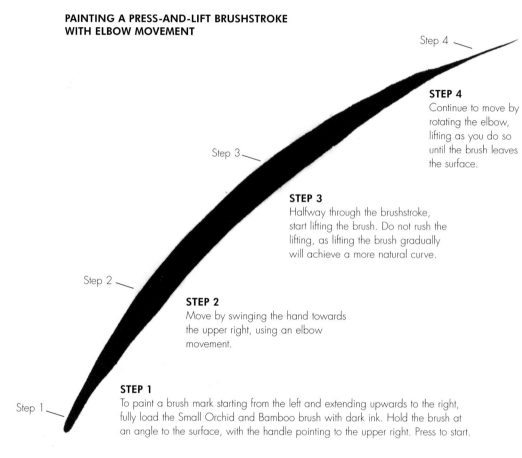

Step 4

STEP 4
Continue to move by rotating the elbow, lifting as you do so until the brush leaves the surface.

Step 3

STEP 3
Halfway through the brushstroke, start lifting the brush. Do not rush the lifting, as lifting the brush gradually will achieve a more natural curve.

Step 2

STEP 2
Move by swinging the hand towards the upper right, using an elbow movement.

Step 1

STEP 1
To paint a brush mark starting from the left and extending upwards to the right, fully load the Small Orchid and Bamboo brush with dark ink. Hold the brush at an angle to the surface, with the handle pointing to the upper right. Press to start.

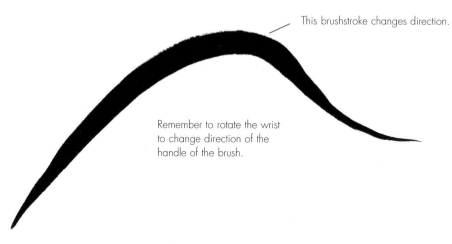

This brushstroke changes direction.

Remember to rotate the wrist to change direction of the handle of the brush.

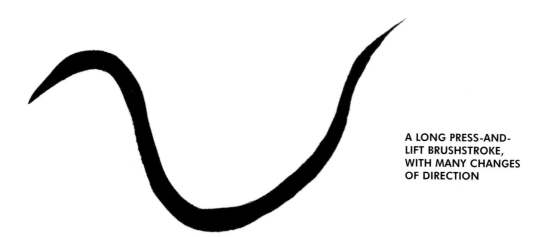

A LONG PRESS-AND-LIFT BRUSHSTROKE, WITH MANY CHANGES OF DIRECTION

For a very long press-and-lift brushstroke, such as the one used for the long, wriggling body of a snake, it is more convenient to use a large brush because you can load more colour on to the brush to sustain a longer brushstroke. If you are using a smaller brush, the colour on the brush may run out and you will have to reload the brush halfway through painting. I painted this brushstroke with the large Bear-hair brush. However, remember to keep moving the brush at a steady speed. If you let the brush stay in one spot for too long, the paper will absorb moisture from the big brush and the colour will bleed beyond control.

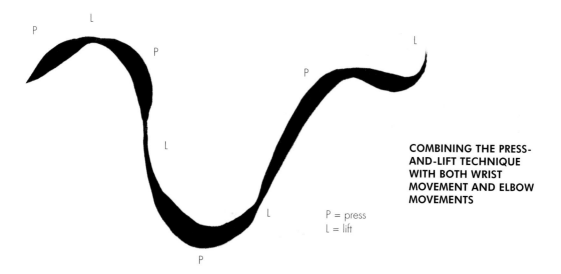

COMBINING THE PRESS-AND-LIFT TECHNIQUE WITH BOTH WRIST MOVEMENT AND ELBOW MOVEMENTS

P = press
L = lift

This long brushstroke is made up of long and short press-and-lift brushstrokes at different intervals. Use wrist movements for the short strokes and elbow movements for the long ones. You will use this type of brushstroke very often when painting animals: for example, to paint the pattern on an animal's body.

EXERCISES

Press-and-lift brushwork is essential to the non-outline style of animal painting. Almost every brushstroke used for building the body involves the press-and-lift technique. Here are some exercises to help get you used to painting animals with the techniques described in this session.

RABBIT'S EARS
I used a Small Orchid and Bamboo brush, fully loaded with ink, to paint each ear, using press-and-lift brushstrokes combined with wrist movement.

HORSE'S TAIL
A simple press-and-lift brushstroke with elbow movement, made with a small Mountain and Horse brush and ink, creates a horse's tail.

TIGER'S BODY MARKINGS
The marks on a tiger's body vary in width and length. I used a combination of wrist and elbow movements, together with the press-and-lift technique, to create a range of markings.

USING BRUSHES ON THEIR SIDE

When you hold the brush at a low angle to the paper, the side of the brush tip touches the paper. Using the side of the brush is popular in painting because this enables the brush to cover a wider area. By holding the brush at different low angles to the paper, we can create different sizes of side brushstrokes. The range can be extended further by using different sizes of brush. The key to using this session to the full is not to restrict yourself simply to the brush I have suggested for an illustration, but to experiment with brushes of other sizes.

The brushstrokes I am going to show you in this session are long dots, extended long dots, straight side brushstrokes, curved side brushstrokes, side brushstrokes made with the press-and-lift technique, fan brushstrokes and reverse fan brushstrokes. It is important to bear in mind that if you load you brush with either two or more tones of the same colour or two or more different colours, the effect you make very much depends on where you place the nib of your brush. Usually it is more convenient to load the darker tone or the darker colour on to the nib of the brush, so you must be sure you know exactly where you want to place the darker tone or colour before you press your brush on the paper.

PAINTING DOTS

LONG DOTS

Fully load a brush with ink. Holding the brush at a low angle to the paper, so that the side of the brush tip is touching the paper, press the brush. The resulting mark has a narrow end where the nib of the brush touches the paper and a wider end where the neck touches the paper. We call this mark a long dot.

**PAINTING A
LONG DOT**

Painting surface

Fully load the Small Orchid and Bamboo brush with ink. Hold the brush at a low angle to the paper and paint a long dot. In this illustration, I held the brush with the nib of the brush pointing to the left, so the resulting mark narrows to the left.

A long dot

DIFFERENT SHAPES OF LONG DOTS

By adjusting the position of the nib of the brush, you can create long dots of different shapes. The narrow end is always where the nib of the brush touches the paper.

The length of a long dot depends on the final angle between brush and paper. The lower the angle, the longer the long dot will be.

A shorter 'long dot' is made when the brush is held at a higher angle.

When the brush is held at a lower angle, the dot is longer.

Long dots can be used for filling spaces and for building shapes. Because a long dot has a narrow end and a wide end, you can manoeuvre either one long dot or multiple dots to fit in any spare space that needs to be filled, which makes them especially useful when you need extra brushstrokes to finish building a shape. For example, in painting the head of a snake, two long dots are added to each side of the initial brushstroke to create the triangular shape of the head.

The triangular head of a snake.

EXTENDED LONG DOTS

If you slide the brush when you are painting a long dot in the direction in which the handle of the brush is pointing, the dot becomes even longer. We call this brush mark an extended long dot. Using wrist movement to slide results in a relatively short extended long dot, while elbow movement makes a longer extended long dot. This brushstroke is frequently used to paint the tails and legs of animals. If you are painting an extended long dot with elbow movement, it is more convenient to use a large brush, as this can hold more colour and therefore go a longer way.

PAINTING AN EXTENDED LONG DOT

Slide the brush in the direction in which the handle is pointing.

An extended long dot using wrist movement.

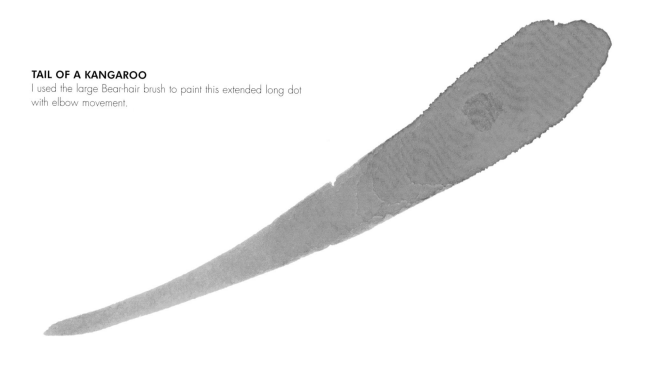

TAIL OF A KANGAROO
I used the large Bear-hair brush to paint this extended long dot with elbow movement.

Multiple long or extended long dots are frequently used to build up large areas of brushwork. Sometimes one brushstroke made with the large Bear-hair brush can create the desired effect, but some areas in animal painting are very large and you have to use more than one brushstroke to build them up, even when you are using a large brush.

A large long dot using the large Bear-hair brush.

Using a few extended long dots to build up a larger area of brushwork.

SIDE BRUSHSTROKES

When you press a brush, the resulting brushwork will usually be wider, but for painting brushwork even wider than can be achieved just by pressing the brush, side brushstrokes are used. In animal painting, the many versions of side brushstrokes are popularly used for building up the contours of bodies. Side brushstrokes can be straight and vertical, horizontal or at an angle. They can also be curved. You can also combine them with the press-and-lift technique to create press-and-lift side brushstrokes.

Straight side brushstrokes are useful for applying colours to the bodies of animals, especially if they are large. Straight side brushstrokes can be vertical, horizontal or at an angle.

VERTICAL SIDE BRUSHSTROKES

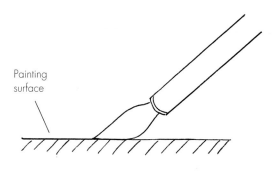

Painting surface

CREATING A VERTICAL SIDE BRUSHSTROKE

STEP 1
Fully load a brush with ink or colour. Hold the brush at an angle to the paper, with the handle pointing to the left or right. The brush is now lying on the side of the brush tip. Press the brush tip on the paper.

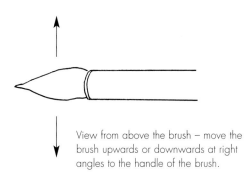

View from above the brush – move the brush upwards or downwards at right angles to the handle of the brush.

STEP 2
Move the brush upwards or downwards at right angles to the handle of the brush to paint a side brushstroke. The brushwork created by moving the brush upwards is similar in shape to the one created by moving the brush downwards.

A vertical side brushstroke using wrist movement with the brush held low to the paper
The angle of the brush to the paper affects the width of the resulting side brushstrokes. The lower the angle, the wider the brushstroke because there is more contact between the brush and the paper. Conversely, the higher the angle, the narrower the brushstroke because there is less contact. The length of a side brushstroke is shorter when you use wrist movement, as shown, and longer when you use elbow movement (see below).

A vertical side brushstroke using wrist movement, with the brush held at a high angle to the paper

A vertical side brushstroke using elbow movement, with the brush held at a low angle to the paper
If you are loading the brush with only one tone of a colour to paint a vertical side brushstroke, the result will be the same, whether you point the nib of the brush to the left or to the right. However, if you load the brush with two tones of a single colour or two colours, the colour arrangements of the resulting brushwork will depend on where you load the darker tone or the darker colour on to the brush. It is more convenient to load the darker tone or the darker colour on to the nib of the brush, which means that when you paint with two tones and two colours, the darker tone or the darker colour will appear where the nib of the brush touches the paper.

A vertical side brushstroke with two tones of a colour
I fully loaded the Small Orchid and Bamboo brush with diluted burnt sienna and dipped the nib of the brush into undiluted burnt sienna. I positioned the nib of the brush to point to the left at a low angle to the paper and painted a side brushstroke with elbow movement.

A vertical side brushstroke with two colours
I fully loaded the Small Orchid and Bamboo brush with burnt sienna and dipped the nib of the brush into ink. I positioned the tip of the brush to point to the left, at a low angle to the paper, and painted a side brushstroke with wrist movement.

HORIZONTAL SIDE BRUSHSTROKES

Hold the brush at an angle to the paper, with the handle of the brush pointing either away from you or towards you. The brush tip is at a vertical position when you view it from above the brush. Move the brush sideways to the left or right in a straight direction. The results are horizontal side brushstrokes.

Again, the width of a horizontal side brushstroke depends on the angle at which you hold your brush to the paper and the length depends on whether you use wrist movement or elbow movement.

You can create straight side brushstrokes pointing in different directions as long as you move the brush tip at right angles to the direction of the handle. If you are using two-tone or two-colour loading, with the darker tone or colour at the nib of the brush, the darker tone or colour will appear where the nib touches the paper.

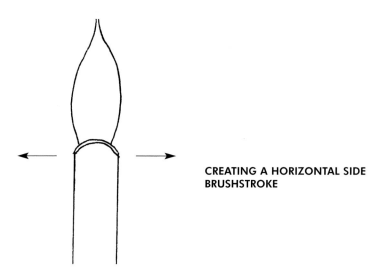

CREATING A HORIZONTAL SIDE BRUSHSTROKE

View from above the brush – move the brush to the right or to the left in a straight line, at right angles to the handle of the brush.

A horizontal side brushstroke using wrist movement, with the brush at a high angle to the paper

A straight side brushstroke at an angle using elbow movement, with the brush at a low angle to the paper

A horizontal side brushstroke with two tones of a colour
I fully loaded the Small Orchid and Bamboo brush with diluted burnt sienna and dipped the nib of the brush into burnt sienna. I positioned the handle of the brush to point towards me at a low angle to the paper and painted a side brushstroke with elbow movement.

A side brushstroke at an angle with two colours
I fully loaded the small Mountain and Horse brush with burnt sienna and dipped the nib of the brush into ink. I positioned the handle of the brush to point at an angle halfway between the right and upwards directions, with the brush tip at a low angle to the paper, and painted a side brushstroke with wrist movement.

CURVED SIDE BRUSHSTROKES

Hold the brush as if you were going to paint a horizontal side brushstroke, but instead of moving the brush in a straight line, move the brush in a curve. The result is a curved side brushstroke. If you use wrist movement, the curve is shorter. The curve is longer if you use an elbow movement. The width of the curved side brushstroke depends on the angle of the brush to the paper. Curved side brushstrokes are very useful for applying colours to the body of an animal, as the majority of animals have curved bodies. When you apply colours to a body, place the nib of the brush on the outline of the body and paint the side brushstrokes, with the nib following the outline.

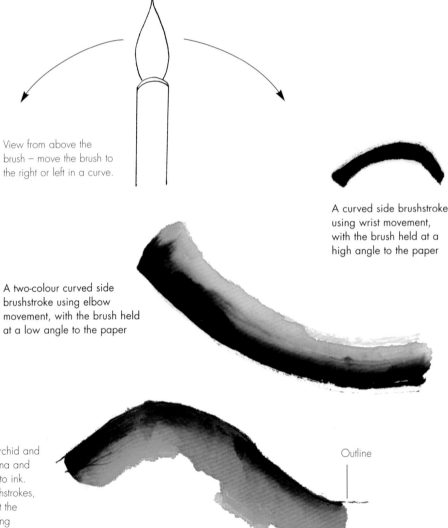

CREATING A CURVED SIDE BRUSHSTROKE

View from above the brush – move the brush to the right or left in a curve.

A curved side brushstroke using wrist movement, with the brush held at a high angle to the paper

A two-colour curved side brushstroke using elbow movement, with the brush held at a low angle to the paper

Applying colours to a body
I used a fully loaded Small Orchid and Bamboo brush with burnt sienna and dipped the nib of the brush into ink. Then I made curved side brushstrokes, placing the nib of the brush at the outline of the body and painting brushstrokes along the outline.

Outline

SIDE BRUSHSTROKES USING PRESS AND LIFT

If you press the brush to begin a side brushstroke and lift to finish, the side brushstroke has a wider end where you press the brush and a narrow end where you lift it. We use press-and-lift side brushstrokes when we have to fit in an area with particular shape. For example, the upper part of the leg of an animal is wider than the lower end. So you start by pressing the brush at the wide end and lifting at the narrow end.

A press-and-lift vertical side brushstroke using wrist movement, with the brush held at a high angle to the paper

A two-tone press-and-lift horizontal side brushstroke using elbow movement, with the brush held at a low angle to the paper

A press-and-lift side brushstroke at an angle

EXERCISES

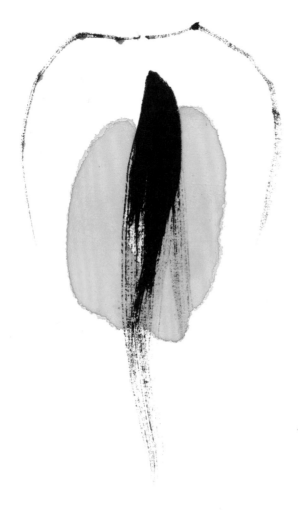

REAR END OF A HORSE
The body of an animal is very often curved.
Here, I have used curved side brushstrokes to
apply colour to the horse. I began by
applying diluted burnt sienna to the inner part
of the hindquarters. Then I loaded the brush
with burnt sienna and dipped the nib of the
brush in ink. I placed the nib of the brush at
the outline of the hindquarters and painted a
long curved side brushstroke along the outline
to finish colouring.

AN ELEPHANT'S LEG
I used the small Mountain and Horse brush and two colours, burnt sienna and burnt sienna darkened with a little bit of ink, to colour this elephant's leg. I started with a vertical side brushstroke, using burnt sienna, and added another vertical side brushstroke with the darkened burnt sienna, overlapping the two colours a little.

A MONKEY'S ARM
I painted the arm of this monkey with a curved side brushstroke, using the small Mountain and Horse brush, with burnt sienna.

LEGS OF A DONKEY
I used two press-and-lift side brushstrokes to colour the legs with the No.3 Leopard and Wolf brush.

FAN BRUSHSTROKES

The length of a fan brushstroke or a reverse fan brushstroke varies according to the angle between the brush and the paper: the lower the angle, the longer the brushwork. However, it is more effective to use different sizes of brush to create different lengths of this brushstroke. You can control the width of the fan brushstroke by how far you move the neck of the brush, but the width of a reverse fan brushstroke is controlled by how far you move the tip of the brush. A small movement results in a narrow brushstroke, while a bigger movement makes a wider brushstroke.

You can start a fan brushstroke or a reverse fan brushstroke from the left or from the right and move in the opposite direction. Either way, the result will be the same.

PAINTING A FAN BRUSHSTROKE

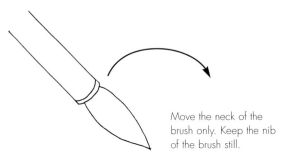

Move the neck of the brush only. Keep the nib of the brush still.

STEP 1
Fully load the No.3 Leopard and Wolf brush with ink or colour and hold the brush at a low angle to the paper.

STEP 2
Using the wrist movement, move the neck of the brush only and keep the nib of the brush still. The resulting brushwork is fan-shaped.

A narrow fan brushstroke, made with a small movement of the neck of the brush.

Nib position

A bigger movement of the neck of the brush results in a wider brushstroke.

Nib position

A fan brushstroke with two colours
Fully load the No.3 Leopard and Wolf brush with burnt sienna and dip the nib of the brush into ink. Hold the brush at a low angle to the paper, with the handle pointing towards you. Paint a fan brushstroke.

Multiple fan brushstrokes
Load the No.3 Leopard and Wolf brush with burnt sienna and dip the nib of the brush into the ink. Paint a few fan brushstrokes side by side to make a bigger area of brushwork. When painting animals, you will generally need more than one fan brushstroke to make up an area of brushwork.

A large fan brushstroke, made with the large Bear-hair brush
You can use the large Bear-hair brush to paint larger fan brushstrokes. Load the large Bear-hair brush with burnt sienna and dip the nib of the brush into ink. Paint a fan brushstroke. Some areas of brushwork are very large, however, and you need more than one fan brushstroke to construct these, even with the large Bear-hair brush.

PAINTING A REVERSE FAN BRUSHSTROKE

Wrist movement is again used to paint a reverse fan brushstroke, but instead of moving the neck of the brush, we move the nib of the brush and keep the neck of the brush still. In animal painting, reverse fan brushstrokes are used more often than fan brushstrokes. Again, you can start a reverse fan brushstroke from the right or from the left and the result will be the same.

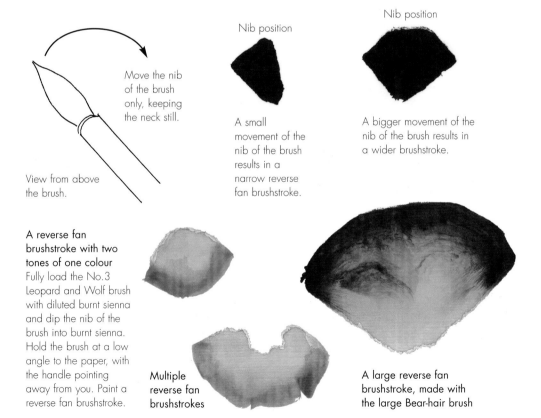

Move the nib of the brush only, keeping the neck still.

View from above the brush.

Nib position

A small movement of the nib of the brush results in a narrow reverse fan brushstroke.

Nib position

A bigger movement of the nib of the brush results in a wider brushstroke.

A reverse fan brushstroke with two tones of one colour
Fully load the No.3 Leopard and Wolf brush with diluted burnt sienna and dip the nib of the brush into burnt sienna. Hold the brush at a low angle to the paper, with the handle pointing away from you. Paint a reverse fan brushstroke.

Multiple reverse fan brushstrokes

A large reverse fan brushstroke, made with the large Bear-hair brush

EXERCISES

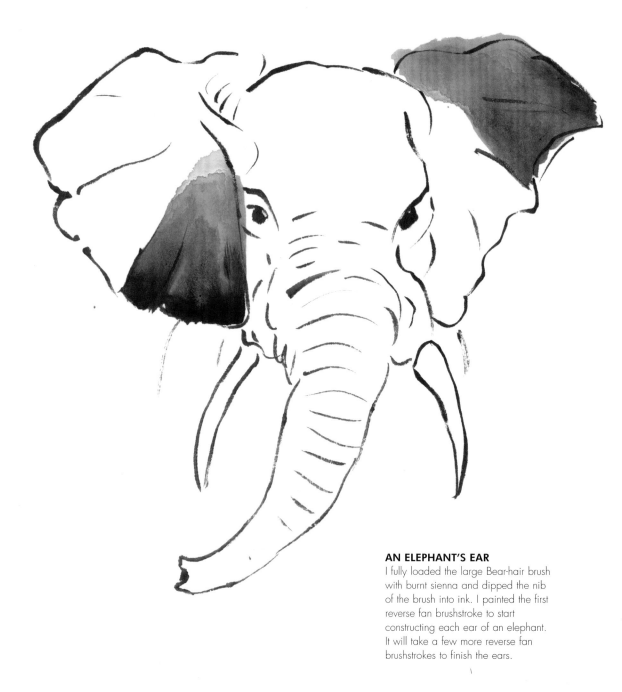

AN ELEPHANT'S EAR
I fully loaded the large Bear-hair brush with burnt sienna and dipped the nib of the brush into ink. I painted the first reverse fan brushstroke to start constructing each ear of an elephant. It will take a few more reverse fan brushstrokes to finish the ears.

PANDA'S EAR
I used multiple fan brushstrokes to paint the ears of a panda with the Small Orchid and Bamboo brush.

SHOULDER MUSCLE
Fan or reverse fan brushstrokes are often used to construct an animal's shoulder muscles.

WET AND DRY BRUSHWORK

Wet and dry brushwork, used separately or together, produce amazing techniques for painting animals. In both cases, the amount of dryness and wetness is carefully controlled to create a range of varied effects. Different brushes are also used to expand the range, offering you a selection of wet or dry brushwork to suit any animal. I am going to give you a brief introduction to these forms of brushwork in this session. You will be guided through the more elaborate techniques step by step in the next chapter.

WET BRUSHWORK

When you fully load a brush with colour and paint on absorbent paper, the resulting brushwork runs. In painting animals, wet brushwork is essential when creating effects of toning and fur.

TONING

If two areas of wet brushwork of different tones of a colour are painted closely together so they overlap a little bit, the two tones will run into each other to create the effect of gradual toning from one into the other. The same happens if two wet areas of different colours are painted close to each other and overlap a little bit. The toning technique can be extended to more than two or three tones or colours, but we shall discuss the more complicated toning techniques in the next chapter.

Usually, if you are creating tones in a narrow area, you can use the technique of two-tone loading in the same brush to cover the area. To create tones in a wider area, it is more efficient to use the techniques mentioned in this section.

In the following illustrations, I have used the Small Orchid and Bamboo brush to paint strips of colour with horizontal side brushstrokes.

Two wet brushstrokes of different tones of burnt sienna, painted so they overlap slightly.

Two wet brushstrokes, one of cadmium orange and the other burnt sienna, painted to overlap slightly.

Three wet brushstrokes, of three different tones of burnt sienna, painted to overlap slightly, create gradual toning.
The most diluted tone was painted first, with a less diluted tone in the middle, followed by the darkest tone.

Three wet brushstrokes, of three different colours, painted to overlap slightly.

FUR

If you apply brushwork to a wet surface, the brushwork will run, creating a fluffy effect. This is the basic principle for creating soft fur. Here are some of the more popular techniques for creating fur effects.

Thick, dark-coloured brushwork on a wet surface

If you apply thick, dark-coloured brushwork to a wet surface, the dark colour will run at the edges to create a fur-like effect. The dark colour will not diffuse into the wet background because the colour is thick. Effects of this type are especially popular for painting the furs of predators.

In the illustration above, I used the small Mountain and Horse brush, fully loaded with dark ink that had been left in the open for some time to thicken. I then painted press-and-lift brushstrokes on to a wet surface coloured with cadmium orange to create the stripes of a tiger's body.

Softer effect, using wetter colours

For a softer effect, such as the fur of a cat, use wetter colours on a wet surface. The wet colours will diffuse into the wet surface, creating a softer impression. In this illustration, I used ink that had just been poured out of the bottle and had not yet thickened to paint the stripes on a wash of burnt sienna.

Very soft fur, using diluted colours

To paint the soft, striped tail of a lesser panda (page 159), I used a diluted colour to paint the pattern on a wet surface. Diluted colours diffuse more than thick colours, creating a softer effect.

I prepared a burnt sienna and a reddish burnt sienna, made by adding alizarin crimson to burnt sienna. I then diluted both colours. I used a large Bear-hair brush, fully loaded with diluted burnt sienna, to paint the tail with a long side brushstroke. I then added the stripes with the diluted reddish burnt sienna.

DRY BRUSHWORK

Dry brushwork is popular in animal painting. The following are the two methods I used to create dry brushwork in this book.

METHOD ONE

When you load a brush with wet paint and wipe off excess moisture on a tissue or a paper towel, the brush becomes a dry brush. The resulting brushwork will have broken, dry patches, so we call this dry brushwork. In general painting, this is how you use most brushes to create dry brushwork. However, the hairs of a Mountain and Horse brush do not carry much moisture, as this particular brush is designed to create dry brushwork naturally. With this brush, therefore, all you need to do to prepare it for creating dry brushwork is just to wipe it against the side of the palette to remove the excess moisture.

A dry press-and-lift ink brushstroke with elbow movement, using the Small Orchid and Bamboo brush.

A dry brushstroke using the press-and-lift technique, made with the Small Mountain and Horse brush.

METHOD TWO

Here, the brush is dry before painting. Different brushes create different effects with dry brushwork. For example, a wolf-hair brush makes softer brushwork than a horse-hair brush, which creates a harder look. A brush with a smaller tip makes narrower brushwork. It also makes shorter brushstrokes because it can only carry a limited amount of colour. A large brush, on the other hand, can make longer and wider brushstrokes.

One of the most common forms of dry brushwork is 'broken brushstrokes'. Here, a dry brush is pressed on the palette before or after being loaded with colour so that the hairs of the brush tip separate before painting. I shall deal with this technique in full detail in the next chapter, where we shall elaborate on the use of dry brushwork and develop further techniques. Before we can do this, however, we must first understand the basic principles of dry brushwork.

Dip the tip of a dry small Landscape brush into ink. Press the tip on the palette until the hairs separate. Paint a brushstroke. This brushstroke is soft, short and narrow.

Dip the brush tip of a dry small Mountain and Horse brush into ink. Press the brush tip on the palette until the hairs separate. Paint a brushstroke. This brushstroke is harder, longer and wider.

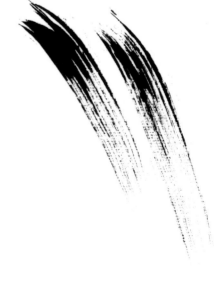

EXERCISES

TAIL OF A HORSE
Load the small Mountain and Horse brush with ink. Wipe off excess ink on the side of the ink server and paint a press-and-lift brushstroke to create the tail of a horse.

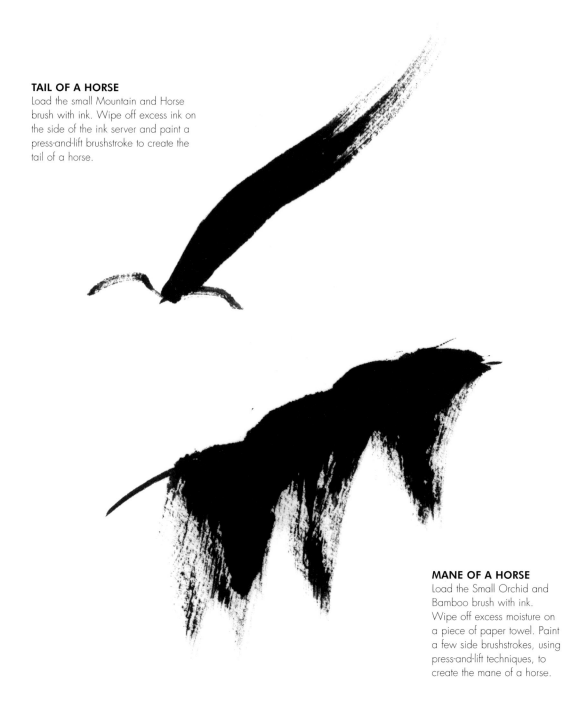

MANE OF A HORSE
Load the Small Orchid and Bamboo brush with ink. Wipe off excess moisture on a piece of paper towel. Paint a few side brushstrokes, using press-and-lift techniques, to create the mane of a horse.

TAIL OF A SQUIRREL
Dip the tip of a dry large
Landscape brush into ink.
Press the brush on the
palette until the hairs
separate. Use this dry brush
to draw the tail of a
squirrel. Notice how soft
such brushwork can be.

3 PAINTING ANIMALS

It is important to get the shape and proportions right when painting an animal. The outline sketches in the opening session of this chapter are designed to help you practise this before you embark on more complex techniques. Each session following the outline sketches concentrates on a particular style. I shall begin the session with instructions that will help you to develop the brushstrokes required to paint in that style. It will be worth spending a little time going through the instructions before you tackle painting the animals properly.

OUTLINE SKETCHES

When painting animals, it is important to get the shapes right. Sketching enables you to practise this, so the first step for anyone wanting to paint animals is to sketch them. Sketch as often as possible. Make use of real-life animals: your own pets, other people's pets, animals in the zoo and pictures in magazines and videos, as well as photos you have taken. Simple sketches with flowing brushstrokes are attractive in their own right. You can add colours to your sketches informally, but do not use too much colour or you will spoil the simplicity of your artworks. There is no reason why you cannot sketch with pencils. I often use pencils for sketching, especially if I am working outdoors. Many people have told me that ancient masters did not sketch with pencils, but that is only because pencils had not then been invented. Modern Chinese masters use them a lot. If you are sketching with pencils on Xuan paper, avoid using an eraser too often because the rubbing will spoil the surface of your paper. Try to sketch with Chinese brushes as well, because you want to be able to draw fluently with these.

HIPPOPOTAMUS
I drew the head of this hippopotamus with the Red Bean brush because I find lines created by the Outline brush too thin for the tough features of a hippopotamus.

DORMOUSE

If you do not have much experience with sketching, you may not be happy with your first drawing. Don't give up. Try again. I usually have to try five or six times before I am satisfied with a sketch. For the dormouse in this illustration, use wrist movements for shorter lines and elbow movements for the longer lines. I used the Red Bean brush here. You might also try using the Outline brush for the dormouse and the Red Bean brush for the branches. If you are using the Red Bean brush, remember to start with the brush dry and dip only the nib into ink when drawing thin lines.

SKETCHES WITH INK

I normally use the Red Bean brush and ink for sketches. Smaller brushes will not carry sufficient ink to sustain a long line. Keep the brush on the dry side. If the brush is wet, it will help to wipe it on a piece of paper towel. Load only the nib of the brush with ink. A fully loaded brush carries too much moisture and the lines you draw will be much thicker. If you want thin lines, hold your brush in a vertical position to draw. Use wrist and elbow movements to make your lines more expressive. You can also use press-and-lift to vary the thickness of the lines. When you are drawing the delicate features of the face, you can use the Outline brush. Use the cushion method for extra support. You can vary the tones of ink to make your sketches more interesting. Sketching is good for practising wrist and elbow movements. These practice sessions will prepare you for the more advanced techniques, in which we shall use both movements a great deal.

LIONS
I used the Red Bean brush to sketch mother and cub, using the press-and-lift technique to draw the lioness, especially her muscles, because this technique makes muscles look tough.

GIRAFFE
I used the Red Bean brush and dark ink to draw the head and neck of this giraffe. Again, I used the press-and-lift technique to emphasize the toughness of the giraffe's muscles. I then used medium ink to add the patterns. Larger patches of pattern are created by painting short lines close together.

TERRIER
I used dark ink with the Red Bean brush to start drawing the overall frame of the terrier. Then I dipped the tip of the Outline brush into diluted ink, adding hairs to create a softer impression.

SKETCHES WITH INK AND COLOUR

If you like, you can add colours informally to your sketches to make them more interesting. You can use the Small Orchid and Bamboo brush, the No.3 Leopard and Wolf brush or the large Bear-hair brush to apply colours, depending on the size of the colour patches. Remember that too wet a brush will cause the colours to run madly. Two practices will help you to control the spread of colours. One is always to start with your brush on the dry side. Wipe it on a piece of paper towel to remove excess moisture from the brush before loading colours. The other is to make your colours a bit thicker than usual. I usually use about three parts of water to two parts of colour from the tube.

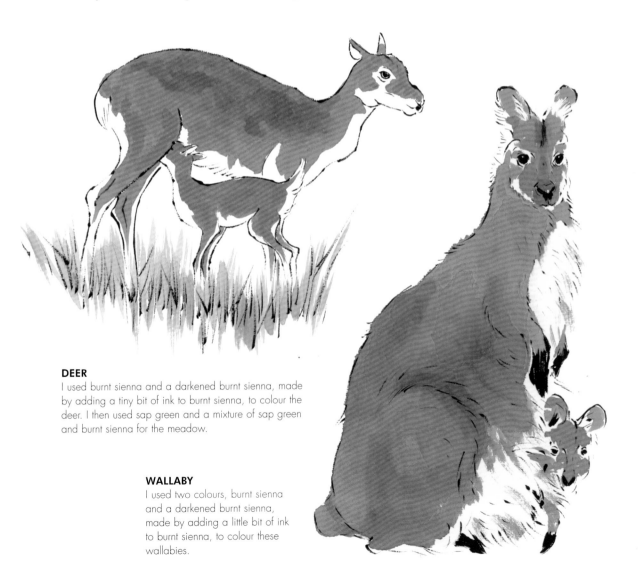

DEER
I used burnt sienna and a darkened burnt sienna, made by adding a tiny bit of ink to burnt sienna, to colour the deer. I then used sap green and a mixture of sap green and burnt sienna for the meadow.

WALLABY
I used two colours, burnt sienna and a darkened burnt sienna, made by adding a little bit of ink to burnt sienna, to colour these wallabies.

MONKEYS
These are snow monkeys.
A touch of alizarin crimson
will be sufficient to highlight
their faces.

RED SQUIRREL
I added alizarin crimson to burnt sienna to
make it reddish. The amount of alizarin
crimson is optional, depending on how red
you want the burnt sienna to be. I then set
aside a portion of the reddish burnt sienna
and darkened it with a tiny bit of ink.
I used these two mixtures to paint the
squirrel.

CAT
This cat has patches of cadmium orange and ink on her back. I used gamboge for her eye.

USING BASIC BRUSHSTROKES

Basic brushstrokes are the results of basic techniques: press-and-lift with wrist movement, press-and-lift with elbow movement, side brushstroke and side brushstroke with press and lift. Every brushstroke has its specific shape. You can combine two or more basic brushstrokes to create complex shapes and build up an image of an animal, and at the same time bring out its character. For example, a long vertical side brushstroke illustrates the straight neck of a horse. A long curved side brushstroke shapes a curved tummy, while you can combine press-and-lift with elbow movement to shape a long leg. The key is to use your brush in a flexible way and be creative: use those brushstrokes that are already available, but when you cannot find any to suit your purpose, create new ones by elaborating on the basic techniques.

Before we begin to paint animals, let me remind you of some of the more commonly used brushstrokes. At the same time, I shall show you how to extend some of them to form new ones.

BRUSHSTROKE 1
A basic press-and-lift brushstroke combined with wrist movement is useful for filling spaces. Here, I am using it to paint the ears of a rabbit.

BRUSHSTROKE 2
A long press-and-lift brushstroke using elbow movement is good for painting a long body or tail. A long press-and-lift brushstroke need not be straight. If you change the direction of the handle of the brush, the long brushstroke will be curved. I am using this brushstroke to paint a tail of a horse.

BRUSHSTROKE 3
You can press and lift more than once to produce a long brushstroke with narrow and wide intervals. I am using it to paint the leg of a donkey.

BRUSHSTROKE 4
Long dots can be used for filling spaces and for building shapes. Multiple long dots can be used to build up a large brushstroke. Here I am using multiple long dots to paint the ears of a panda.

BRUSHSTROKE 5
Extended long dots are very often used to shape tails and legs. Here, I am using an extended long dot to paint the tail of a kangaroo.

BRUSHSTROKE 6
Straight side brushstrokes are effective for painting straight features, such as a neck or a leg. Multiple straight side brushstrokes are useful for covering a large area, such as the body of an animal. Here I am using it to paint the neck of a horse.

BRUSHSTROKE 8
Long and short curved side brushstrokes are used for filling spaces along a curve. They are also used for creating shoulder muscles. In this illustration, I am using the brushstroke to colour the lower abdomen of a horse.

BRUSHSTROKE 7
Press-and-lift side brushstrokes, upwards or downwards, are useful for painting the legs of animals.

BRUSHSTROKE 9
Variation 1: Lay the brush on its side with the handle pointing to the right. Move the brush tip to the right and downward and then to the left.

Variation 2: Lay the brush on its side with the handle pointing to the left. Move the brush tip to the left and downward and then to the right.

Variation 3: Lay the brush on its side with the handle pointing to the right. Move the brush to the right then downward.

Variation 4: Lay the brush on its side with the handle pointing to the left. Move the brush to the left then downward.

USING SINGLE BRUSHSTROKES

I am starting with a few simple animals. The body of each of these can be created with a single brushstroke. You have to manoeuvre the brush, using the press-and-lift technique and wrist and elbow movements to create the shape of the body.

COLOURS
- Ink
- Burnt sienna
- Process white
- Permanent rose

BRUSHES
- Large Bear-hair brush
- Red Bean brush
- Outline brush
- No.1 Wolf-hair brush for Painting

RAT

The rat is a lucky animal in the Chinese calendar so Chinese artists like to paint rats. Many people may not like rats and mice, but painting them is a good way to practise your brushstrokes. Rats are bigger and mice are smaller, but essentially they have the same shape. The body of a rat or a mouse can be created using a single long dot, with either ink or burnt sienna darkened with a tiny bit of dark ink.

STEP 1

Prepare a darkened burnt sienna by adding a little bit of ink to burnt sienna. Fully load the large Bear-hair brush. Paint a long dot for the body.

STEP 2

Mix permanent rose with a little bit of burnt sienna. Dip the Red Bean brush into this mixture and add the tail.

STEP 3

Dip the Outline brush into dark ink. Draw the feet and eyes and add details to the body and the tail. Dip the No.1 Wolf-hair brush into process white and add the details to the eyes and the ears.

A RAT
I used an extended long dot for the right-hand rat, manoeuvring the brush to change direction in the middle of the dot.

LIZARD

You can create the body of a lizard with one single brushstroke, using the press-and-lift technique as described here.

STEP 1

Load the Small Orchid and Bamboo brush with burnt sienna. Use a single brushstroke to paint the body. You can start from the head or the tail (I started from the head). Press to widen the brushstroke to paint the body, and then gradually lift the brush to finish with the tail. Change the direction of the brushstroke according to the movement of the body (refer to Brushstroke 3 on page 84). If you start painting from the tail, hold your brush at an angle to the paper with only the nib of the brush touching the paper. Slowly press the brush as you paint the tail, then the body, finally lifting a little to form the head. Always adjust the handle of the brush to point in the direction of your painting movement.

STEP 2

When the colour is dry, add the legs with burnt sienna. Draw the body pattern, using the Red Bean brush loaded with ink and process white.

COLOURS
• Ink
• Burnt sienna
• Process white

BRUSHES
• Small Orchid and Bamboo brush
• Red Bean brush

Step 1   Step 2

COLOURS
- Ink
- Sap green
- Process white
- Cadmium red

BRUSHES
- Large Bear-hair brush
- Small Orchid and Bamboo brush
- Red Bean brush
- No.1 Wolf-hair brush for Painting

SNAKE

Use a large brush because more colour can be loaded on to a large brush, which means you can go a longer way. The body of the snake is long. If you use the Small Orchid and Bamboo brush, you may have to reload the brush with colour halfway through painting and you may lose the momentum you need to maintain the correct width of the body. The body is thinner in the part near to the head, but bigger in the middle; it then thins down towards the tail. Press the brush to widen the brushstroke and lift it to thin it. To achieve uniform thickness in the middle part of the body, it is important to maintain a constant pressure on the brush.

STEP 1

Load the large Bear-hair brush with sap green. Paint the long body, using elbow movement and starting with the head. Press when the part of body is wider and lift when it thins down, finally lifting the brush to finish with the tail (see Brushstroke 2 on page 84). Always adjust the handle of the brush to point in the direction of your painting movement.

STEP 2

Use the Small Orchid and Bamboo brush and sap green to add a long dot to each side of the head, creating a triangular shape.

STEP 3

When the colour is dry, dip the No.1 Wolf-hair brush for Painting into cadmium red and paint the tongue. Next, dip the brush into dark ink and draw the scales. Add the eyes and the rest of the pattern with the Red Bean brush, using the appropriate colours.

Step 1

Steps 2
and 3

USING LARGE BRUSHSTROKES

Basically, a large brushstroke is a large patch of colour, usually painted using a large brush. If you are using a smaller brush, you have to use multiple brushstrokes to build it up, using long dots or short press-and-lift brushstrokes, or a mixture of both. For a very large patch of colour, side brushstrokes are best for filling up spaces, and even if you use a large brush, you may still need to make multiple brushstrokes when painting some animals.

PANDA

The panda is practically a symbol of China. A few brushstrokes with ink in a lively style express a panda's shape, movement, character and mood. A panda is made up of large patches of black and white, so you can use ink to paint the black patches with a large brush. To create the white patches, you can leave the spaces blank on the paper.

STEP 1
Use the Red Bean brush and diluted ink to sketch a panda. Carefully mark the dark patches.

STEP 2
Use either the Small Orchid and Bamboo brush or the large Bear-hair brush to paint the dark patches with dark ink. You can use long dots, side brushstrokes or a mixture of both. Sometimes, you may like the patches of colour to convey the feeling of fur. The way to do this is to start at the edge of a patch that you want to fill with colour. Use a smaller brush to paint the fur effect along the edge with small press-and-lift brushstrokes. Then fill the rest of the patch with colour. The illustration on the right shows how to start the press-and-lift brushstrokes on a panda's leg to create a fur effect.

STEP 3
Dip the Red Bean brush into dark ink and draw the outlines to finish. You can add some claws to the paws and also the pupils of the eyes, using process white and the No.1 Wolf-hair brush for Painting. Each panda paw has six digits, but you seldom see all of them. Usually you cannot see the eyes or the digits because they are black, so you only see an outline of them when they catch the reflection of light.

COLOURS
• Ink
• Process white

BRUSHES
• Red Bean brush
• Small Orchid and Bamboo brush or large Bear-hair brush
• No.1 Wolf-hair brush for Painting

Using the press-and-lift technique to suggest fur.

Step 1

Step 2

MORE ANIMALS PAINTED WITH LARGE BRUSHSTROKES

You can also paint a panda on a piece of absorbent paper tinted with a colour wash. Proceed with the same steps as before. When all the ink brushwork is dry, use process white to fill in the white parts of the panda's body.

A panda with bamboo.

A panda mum and her cub.

BLACK DUTCH RABBIT
You can use the panda-painting techniques to paint a Dutch rabbit. Use diluted permanent rose to tint the ears, nose, mouth and feet.

BLACK CAT
If you want to paint a black cat without toning, use multiple brushstrokes to build up the black body of the cat, adding in the details of the face, teeth, paws and whiskers. Work over the black with process white for further detailing, if required.

USING MULTIPLE BRUSHSTROKES

Animals with more complex shapes can be painted with multiple brushstrokes, using different strokes for different parts of the body. The purpose is to create a more three-dimensional figure. Multiple brushstrokes are very popular with animal painters. Theoretically, any animal can be painted with the Chinese brush using multiple brushstrokes. In this session, I will show just a few examples, but I hope you will feel free to use the same techniques to paint animals other than those illustrated.

KANGAROO

I have used only one tone of burnt sienna to paint the kangaroo, but I use a very effective and unique way of toning, which is easy to carry out.

The top diagram on the opposite page identifies all the brushstrokes used for painting the kangaroo. Each number corresponds to the number of a brushstroke from the list on page 84–85. It is only a suggestion, but I hope that this will help you to start getting used to building shapes.

Use the No.3 Leopard and Wolf brush to paint the brushstrokes for the head. Use the Small Orchid and Bamboo brush, the small Mountain and Horse brush and the large Bear-hair brush for the body, selecting your brush according to the size of each brushstroke. Leave a little space between adjacent brushstrokes.

STEP 1
Sketch the outline of a kangaroo with the Red Bean brush and diluted ink. Follow the outline in the diagram. Prepare burnt sienna, darkened with a little bit of ink.

STEP 2
Start by constructing the face and the head, following the brushstrokes in the diagram. Next, use a large brush to paint the tail with an extended long dot. Continue to sweep the extended long dot to form the back. Alternatively, use a separate side brushstroke to paint the back.

STEP 3
Follow the diagram to finish adding all the other brushstrokes. Remember to leave a narrow gap between adjacent brushstrokes.

COLOURS
- Ink
- Darkened burnt sienna, made by adding a tiny bit of ink to burnt sienna

BRUSHES
- Red Bean brush
- No.3 Leopard and Wolf brush
- Small Orchid and Bamboo brush
- Small Mountain and Horse brush
- Large Bear-hair brush
- Outline brush

Brushstroke key
(see pages 84–85)

Steps 1 and 2

Step 3

STEP 4

While the colour is still wet, use a clean No.3 Leopard and Wolf brush to apply clean water to the spaces between brushstrokes, also touching the sides of each brushstroke. The purpose is to soften the edges of the colour and create tones to link muscles together. Leave the colour to dry.

STEP 5

Use the Outline brush and dark ink to add features to the face and to the feet, and then use the Red Bean brush to add outlines wherever these will enhance the general effect. I used dark ink for some outlines and the darkened burnt sienna for others.

Steps 4 and 5

MORE ANIMALS PAINTED USING MULTIPLE BRUSHSTROKES

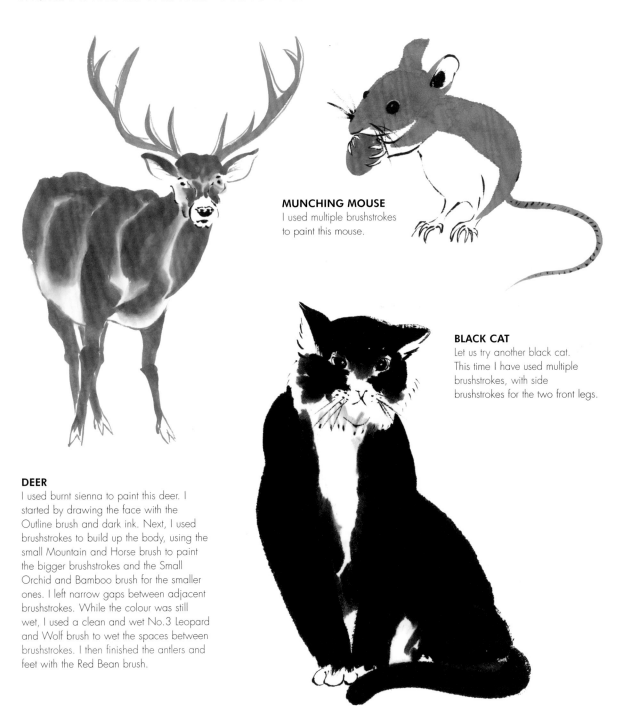

MUNCHING MOUSE
I used multiple brushstrokes
to paint this mouse.

BLACK CAT
Let us try another black cat.
This time I have used multiple
brushstrokes, with side
brushstrokes for the two front legs.

DEER
I used burnt sienna to paint this deer. I
started by drawing the face with the
Outline brush and dark ink. Next, I used
brushstrokes to build up the body, using the
small Mountain and Horse brush to paint
the bigger brushstrokes and the Small
Orchid and Bamboo brush for the smaller
ones. I left narrow gaps between adjacent
brushstrokes. While the colour was still
wet, I used a clean and wet No.3 Leopard
and Wolf brush to wet the spaces between
brushstrokes. I then finished the antlers and
feet with the Red Bean brush.

EXPRESSIVE BRUSHSTROKES

I am sure many readers are very impressed by the expressive way in which artists can depict an entire animal in only a few brushstrokes. The way masters do this appears almost magical, but it need not be so. The key to achieving this style of painting is to use brushstrokes well. Let me demonstrate this beautiful technique with a painting of a cat. You will by now appreciate that we can paint the cat with many basic brushstrokes. However, when you know your brushstrokes really well, you can link a few brushstrokes together and deliver one continuous stroke, without having to lift the brush off the paper. We usually use a large brush for this technique because it can carry more colour and therefore it goes a longer way. A large brush also enables you to achieve a greater range of widths by pressing, lifting and using the brush on its side.

CAT PAINTED WITH BASIC BRUSHSTROKES

The outline of the face is indicated by the diluted ink. I used different brushstrokes to paint the head and side brushstrokes, close together, to paint the body. In the illustration below, I left narrow gaps between brushstrokes to show you the position of each. In a normal painting, you would pack the brushstrokes close together to form larger ones.

Painting the cat in the usual way, with basic brushstrokes.

Step 1

CAT PAINTED WITH EXPRESSIVE BRUSHSTROKES

Now I am going to link brushstrokes together and paint the cat again. It is more convenient to use a large brush to paint a long, continuous brushstroke, so I used a large Bear-hair brush, fully loaded with dark ink. The basic shape of the body was executed in three expressive brushstrokes. The key to linking brushstrokes together to form a continuous one, complete with all the different widths, is to constantly press or lift, changing the angle of the brush to the painting surface, and changing the direction of the brush handle to follow the shape of the body. There is a lot happening in one continuous brushstroke, so you have to be familiar with the shape you are aiming at and be efficient in manoeuvring the brush to construct the shape. It is hard work, but the result is very rewarding.

Step 2

STEP 1

I started the brushstroke at the forehead with a fully loaded large Bear-hair brush. I moved the brush to the top of the head and down to the neck, leaving a space in between to shape the ear. You should press and lift the brush to acquire the necessary width at different places. If you find the large Bear-hair brush too large to handle, you can use the small Mountain and Horse brush for this brushstroke.

STEP 2

Fully load the large Bear-hair brush, again with dark ink. Start with the brush in a vertical position at the neck of the cat. As you move the brush downwards, press and at the same time gradually lower the angle of the brush until you are using the side of the brush to finish the brushstroke.

Step 3

STEP 3

Use the same technique as used for the second brushstroke to paint a third stroke, completing the left half of the body. As you reach the bottom of the body, gradually increase the angle of the brush until the brush is in a vertical position. Press to continue and paint the tail. I added a small press-and-lift brushstroke to paint the other ear and a long dot for the cheek. Then I used the Outline brush to add final details.

MORE ANIMALS PAINTED USING EXPRESSIVE BRUSHSTROKES

SLEEPING CAT
The cat is one of my favourite animals for practising this technique. Note how the whole body was constructed in one brushstroke. I started with the tail, using medium ink. Where the tail joins the body, I lowered the angle of the brush and used side brushstrokes to complete the body. Then I added a long dot of dark ink at the tip of the tail and other details.

RACING HUSKY
I began painting the body with dark ink and then added the diluted ink patches. The other details were added in dark ink with the Outline brush. A little colour for the inner ear and tongue completes the image.

WILY WEASEL

Use a large brush. Starting with the head, manoeuvre the brush with all the basic techniques – press-and-lift, wrist and elbow movements and side brushstrokes – and then continue to paint the neck. When you reach the body, lower the angle of the brush and use side brushstrokes to construct the body. Continue to use side brushstrokes to paint the thigh of the hind leg. Next, rotate your wrist to position the brush at a high angle and finish the lower part of the hind leg. Try to do it all in one go. If you find completing it in one go too ambitious, you can always use different brushstrokes to construct the body. Use the same brush and colour to add the front leg and tail. Add all other details with the Red Bean brush and ink.

PLAYFUL OTTER

I took two brushstrokes to construct the body, using burnt sienna darkened with a little bit of ink. One brushstroke started from the head and the other started from the narrow end of the tail. As each of the brushstrokes lengthened, I gradually lowered the angle of the brush until it was on its side to cover the width of the body.

TWO-TONE AND TWO-COLOUR LOADING

To paint smaller-scale animal artworks with different tones of a colour or different colours, it is more convenient to use two-tone or two-colour loading. I shall demonstrate painting a monkey with these techniques, using multiple brushstrokes. Painting monkeys is fun. They have long arms and legs, so you can paint them with side brushstrokes, using elbow movements. Hold the brush at different angles to the paper to control the width of a side brushstroke. If a stroke needs to be very wide, use two or three brushstrokes to build up the width.

MONKEY

COLOURS
- Ink
- Burnt sienna
- Darkened burnt sienna
- Alizarin crimson

BRUSHES
- Red Bean brush
- Outline brush
- Small Mountain and Horse brush

STEP 1

Draw a sketch of the monkey with the Red Bean brush and burnt sienna. Draw the face with the Outline brush and dark ink.

STEP 2

Prepare burnt sienna and the darkened burnt sienna. Load the small Mountain and Horse brush with burnt sienna and dip the nib of the brush into dark ink. Paint the hair of the head, using press-and-lift brushstrokes.

STEP 3

Fully load the small Mountain and Horse brush with the darkened burnt sienna and paint two straight side brushstrokes to form the arm at the front. When the colour is still wet, dip the Red Bean brush into dark ink and add the fingers. Use multiple side brushstrokes to paint the body. Then add the other arm and two legs. Fully load the small Mountain and Horse brush, again with the darkened burnt sienna, and dip the nib of the brush into dark ink. Holding the brush vertically, paint the tail from the end tip until it finally joins the body. The brush is loaded with two colours, with the dark ink in the nib. If you start from the end tip of the tail, the tip will be dark. As you paint the long tail, the dark ink will slowly run out, leaving the brush with the darkened burnt sienna to join the body, which has the same colour. Use the Red Bean brush and diluted alizarin crimson to colour the face and the inside of the ear.

Steps 1 and 2

Step 3

MORE ANIMALS PAINTED USING TWO-TONE AND TWO-COLOUR LOADING

HAVING A SNACK
This monkey is painted in the same way as the one on the previous page.

A MOMENT TOGETHER
Notice here that the baby is a lighter colour than its mother – I used burnt sienna darkened with ink for the mother.

DONKEY MUM AND FOAL

I used burnt sienna and darkened burnt sienna, made by adding a little bit of ink to the burnt sienna. I started with the foal, using the darkened burnt sienna. When I painted the mother, I first loaded the brush with burnt sienna and then dipped the nib of the brush into the darkened burnt sienna to create tones. I used side brushstrokes most of the time for the bodies. For the legs, I used the press-and-lift technique, pressing the brush at the joints, where they are wider. Use the No.3 Leopard and Wolf brush for small brushstrokes, the small Mountain and Horse brush for large brushstrokes and the Red Bean brush for the finer brushwork and outlines.

RELAXING TOGETHER

The water buffaloes of South East Asia are domesticated and a water buffalo is usually an important member of a farming family because it helps ploughing the fields. Each buffalo usually has a young carer, who scrubs the buffalo in the river after work, feeds it and gets it ready for work in the morning. This illustration shows a lad relaxing on the back of his pal. I prepared burnt sienna and darkened burnt sienna. I then used two-colour loading to paint the head and the body of the water buffalo.

COLOURS
- Ink
- Burnt sienna
- Sap green

BRUSHES
- Large Bear-hair brush or Extra-large Mountain and Horse brush
- Red Bean brush
- Outline brush

PROJECT: RELAXING IN THE BREEZE

The camel is a very popular subject for painting in expressive brushstrokes. The process is really not difficult and is full of fun. You need to use a large brush. I have painted the camels with two humps, as Bactrian camels (with two humps) come from China and Mongolia.

STEP 1

There are two camels in this artwork. To paint the front one, I used three colours: burnt sienna, a burnt sienna darkened by adding a bit of ink, and dark ink. To paint the one in the back, I also used three colours: a darkened burnt sienna, another darkened burnt sienna, darker than the first one, and dark ink. Prepare all three colours for each animal before commencing painting. You need to apply the next colour while the previous colours are still wet. This means that after you apply one colour, you will not have time to prepare the next colour before continuing painting.

STEP 2

Start with the camel shown at the front of the picture opposite. Fully load a large brush with burnt sienna. Start with the face and continue to paint the neck, pressing the brush if you need to. Without stopping, lower the angle of the brush and use a side brushstroke to paint the upper part of the body, continuing to finish the rear end. Still continuing to paint, raise the angle of the brush until it is higher and paint the hind legs. Using the same brush and colour, add the front leg. Now dip the brush into the darkened burnt sienna and paint the lower tummy, using side brushstrokes. Use the same colour to add long dots for the back and front feet. Clean the brush and then fully load it with dark ink. Add the lumps of hair on top of the humps, at the back and front of the neck, on top of the head and top of the front leg. Allow all colours to dry before drawing the tail and the features of the face with dark ink using the outline brush.

STEP 3

Use the same techniques to paint the second camel, but this time start with the lighter darkened burnt sienna, followed by the darker darkened burnt sienna. This camel also has two hind legs to finish.

STEP 4

Prepare three colours: dark ink, sap green and a mixture of one part sap green to one part burnt sienna. Use these to paint lines for the grass with the Red Bean brush.

USING TONING TECHNIQUES

Toning is an essential technique in animal painting. Whether you are painting with ink or with colours, toning techniques can be used to create three-dimensional effects and bring animals to life. You can create toning with two or more tones of a single colour or with two or more colours. The following are a few tips for creating successful toning.

TIPS FOR TONING TECHNIQUES

1   Make sure your brush is fairly dry before loading it with colour. If you use a wet brush, you will upset the delicate balance of the intended tone because the extra moisture in the brush will dilute the colour. Also, the extra moisture will cause the brush marks to expand more than you had planned. So before you load the brush with a colour, wipe it on absorbent paper, such as a paper towel, to get rid of as much moisture as possible.

It is worth mentioning that most Chinese brush artists paint very large paintings. When you paint animals on this scale, using the non-outline style on absorbent paper, you need a lot of moisture. Wet brushes seldom cause colours to bleed beyond the intended outline when you are painting on a large scale. However, when you are painting small-scale animals, any excessive moisture will expand madly. If you make sure your brush is dry before loading it with ink and paint, you will minimize the likelihood of this happening.

2   You may find that it is more convenient to use different sizes of brush to create toning in different areas. For example, use the Red Bean brush for the small parts on the face and the No.3 Leopard and Wolf brush for the legs and arms. For the body, use the Small Orchid and Bamboo brush or a small Mountain and Horse brush. For even larger areas, such as the back of a pig or an elephant, you can use the Extra-large Mountain and Horse brush or the large Bear-hair brush.

3   I always use contrasting dry detailed brushwork with wet, expressive toning. You can paint the details before the expressive toning or vice versa, provided one type of brushwork is dry before you apply the other. The advantage of painting details first is that details dry quickly and you can then go on with toning. If you start with the wet toning areas, you will find you need to wait longer for your work to dry before you can add the details. However, the advantage of painting the toning first is that if the wet areas of toning spread beyond the original outlines, you can adjust the boundaries of the detailing to hide this.

TONING METHODS

There are many toning techniques, but these three methods are the most popular. You can use any of the following methods for painting any animal. You can also combine two or more methods when painting a single animal.

METHOD 1: APPLYING CLEAN WATER FIRST

The simplest way to create two tones is to wet the edge of the area where you are going to apply colour with clean water. Then add colour to the rest of the area, overlapping a little of the clean-water area. The colour will run into the clean water to create gradual tones. When you apply the clean water or colour, do not apply it right to the edge of the intended area. Leave a narrow gap of dry paper between the outline of the area and the application of the water or colour, as the latter will eventually expand. Leaving a dry gap will prevent the wetness expanding too far beyond the intended edges.

STEP 1
The two lines at the top and bottom show the area where you are going to apply colour. I applied clean water to the lower half of the area, leaving a narrow dry gap near to the lower edge. The dark lines indicate the area where water was applied.

Step 1

STEP 2
Apply colour to the upper half, overlapping the clean-water area a little. Again, leave a narrow dry gap between the upper edge and the colour. You can see how the colour expands outwards.

The size of the water patch affects the outcome of the toning: if you apply a thin line of water, the toning will only extend thinly. This can be useful when you paint faces and limbs. If you apply colour to a wider patch of water, it will expand to a wider area. However, because the paper is absorbent, the colour will be absorbed at the same time as it expands. As a result, the colour will not spread to cover the entire wet patch, and the outcome will be a lighter tone next to the colour patch and a blank area in the rest of the wet patch. This effect can be especially useful when you paint the tummy or shoulder of an animal, for which both toning and blank space are required.

Step 2

Creating toning in the tummy area of an animal.

Creating toning on an animal's leg.

METHOD 2: APPLYING DIFFERENT TONES SEPARATELY

You can use this method to apply two or more tones. You begin with one tone of a colour and then apply another tone of the same colour, applying it next to the first one and overlapping the two a little bit. You can go on adding more subtly graded tones next to each other. The easiest way is to start with the most diluted tone and add the next most diluted one. This way, you do not need to rinse your brush. If you were to start with the darkest tone, you would have to rinse your brush clean in order to follow on with a more diluted tone. This is the most popular toning method, because it is so flexible: you can use as many tones or as many colours as you like, and you can cover a large area with this technique. The steps below also apply to multi-coloured toning (you will see more three-colour toning in the section on animals with patterns).

Here, I used three tones of burnt sienna and the Small Orchid and Bamboo brush, painting long straight side brushstrokes with each tone.

STEP 1
Start with the most diluted tone.

STEP 2
Add the next most diluted tone above it, overlapping a little of the most diluted tone.

STEP 3
Add the darkest tone above the other two, again overlapping a little bit of the previous tone.

Step 1

Step 2

Step 3

Variation

Sometimes, when you want the darker tone to be stronger, you need to apply a darker tone before the more diluted one. For example, if you were painting a black horse in different tones of ink, you might want the dark ink to be more distinctive, to express the toughness of the muscles. In this case, the darker tone will be applied first, to indicate the position of the muscles. The dark tone will sink into the absorbent paper before the more diluted tone is added and will stand out, creating the stronger features.

In this illustration, I used toning to paint the shoulder muscle of a horse. I started with the small Mountain and Horse brush and used dark ink to paint a curved side brushstroke. Then I cleaned the brush and dipped it into diluted ink to apply short side brushstrokes, overlapping the dark ink.

Shoulder muscle of a horse

MULTI-COLOURED TONING

Method 2 also works for multi-coloured toning. Again, the usual practice is to apply the lightest colour first, followed by the second lightest colour and so on.

In this illustration, I used cadmium orange, followed by burnt sienna, finishing with burnt sienna darkened with a little bit of ink.

METHOD 3: TWO-TONE OR TWO-COLOUR LOADING

You can load a brush with two tones of the same colour, usually with the darker tone at the nib of the brush. Any resulting brushwork will carry two tones of the colour, the darker tone appearing where the nib of the brush touches the paper. The same principle applies to two-colour loading in a brush. This is an efficient way of applying two tones or colours at the same time. For three-colour toning, it is better to use Method 2.

A side brushstroke, using a brush loaded with two tones of the same colour
I loaded the brush with diluted burnt sienna and dipped the nib into burnt sienna. I then painted a horizontal side brushstroke.

A side brushstroke, using a brush loaded with two colours
I loaded the brush with burnt sienna and dipped the nib into ink. I then painted a horizontal side brushstroke.

COVERING A LARGE AREA WITH TWO-TONE OR TWO-COLOUR LOADING

Your brush may not be large enough to cover the whole of a large area. In this case, you can use two-tone or two-colour loading to cover part of the area, and then extend the colours on each side of the brushstroke. This illustration will give you a clearer idea how this works.

Here, I loaded the Small Orchid and Bamboo brush with burnt sienna and dipped the nib of the brush into ink. I placed the brush nib next to the edge and painted a curved side brushstroke. Then I cleaned the brush and loaded it with burnt sienna to finish colouring the rest of the area beneath the burnt sienna.

COMBINING METHODS

Each of the above three methods can be used on its own, but we very often use more than one method in a single piece of artwork, so I am going to show you how easy it is to combine methods.

COMBINING METHODS 1 AND 2

Start with a long side brushstroke, made with clean water. Add a long side brushstroke above the clean water area, using cadmium orange, and then make another long side brushstroke, this time using burnt sienna. Overlap adjacent brushstrokes.

COMBINING METHODS 1 AND 3

Start with a long side brushstroke, made with clean water. Fully load a brush with burnt sienna and dip the nib of the brush into ink. Paint a long side brushstroke above the clean water area, overlapping it a little bit.

COMBINING METHODS 2 AND 3

Start with a long side brushstroke of diluted burnt sienna. Fully load the brush with burnt sienna, and dip the nib of the brush into ink. Paint a long side brushstroke above the diluted burnt sienna, overlapping it a little bit.

COLOURS
- Ink
- Permanent rose

BRUSHES
- Red Bean brush
- Small Orchid and Bamboo brush
- Small Mountain and Horse brush
- Extra-large Mountain and Horse brush or large Bear-hair brush

PIGS

The pig's body is smooth and does not have many visible muscles. The most effective way to paint a pig is to use a gradual toning of ink. I built up the tones one by one, using Methods 1 and 2 and starting with clean water and then the most diluted tone. When all the ink tones had been applied and had dried, I used a diluted pink to highlight the nose, mouth, ears and trotters.

STEP 1

Draw the outline of a pig with the Red Bean brush and diluted ink, and then make three tones of ink: diluted, medium and dark.

STEP 2

Slightly load the Small Orchid and Bamboo brush with clean water and wet the place where you want to have lighter colour (or leave it blank). Fully load the small Mountain and Horse brush with diluted ink and paint the part next to the clean water with side brushstrokes, allowing the ink to bleed into the clean-water area.

STEP 3

Load the small Mountain and Horse brush with medium ink and continue to add colour to the body, as shown in the illustration.

STEP 4

Fully load the Extra-large Mountain and Horse or the large Bear-hair brush with dark ink. Place the nib of the brush along the upper edge, with the neck of the brush touching the medium ink. Go across with a long side brushstroke, following the outline of the body. Alternatively, you can use the Small Mountain and Horse brush and paint two or three long side brushstrokes. Leave all inked areas to dry. Next, dip the Red Bean brush into dark ink and draw the eyes, nose, the trotters, tail and any outlines you want to add. Use diluted permanent rose to add colour to the nose, ears, mouth and trotters.

Step 1

Step 2

Step 3

STEP 4
My pupils called him the bank manager.
What is your opinion?

ANOTHER PIG
For this illustration, I started with the most diluted ink in the centre of the pig's back. I then moved outwards, adding darker tones of ink.

COLOURS
• Ink

BRUSHES
• Red Bean brush
• Small Mountain and
  Horse brush

HORSES

Many artists favour a complete non-outline approach to horse painting: in other words, they use no outlines at all. I personally like to use outlines for the head and legs, as this makes them more clearly defined and sharp, and hence stronger. Horses are the ultimate test of your ability to express the shape, movement and character of an animal. In this session, I am going to show you how to paint horses in two different ways: one simply with ink and the other with colours.

PAINTING A HORSE WITH INK

Unlike the body of a pig, the body of a horse displays lots of muscles. In order to define these muscles, we use Method 2, but we start the toning with dark ink so that this stands out more clearly. I am going to show you how to paint a black horse, using only ink. In order to convey a three-dimensional effect, you have to use different brushstrokes, with different tones of ink, to create the muscles. This will be a test of your skill.

STEP 1

Dip the Red Bean brush into diluted ink. Holding the brush in an upright position, use the tip to sketch the horse, using wrist movements for short lines and elbow movements for longer lines. Mark the positions of the muscles. This is important, because the application of ink will depend on the position of the muscles. You do not need too many or you will lose the effect, but you must have enough to show the tight body structure. I like to draw the face and the legs with dark ink at this early stage, using the Red Bean brush. I do this to show off the strength of the legs and the elegant features of the face.

STEP 2

Load the small Mountain and Horse brush with dark ink to paint the muscles, joints and also places that are shadowed. Use a straight side brushstroke for the neck, curved side brushstrokes for the body and press-and-lift side brushstrokes for the joints of the legs. Before the dark ink dries, go straight to Step 3.

STEP 3

Clean the small Mountain and Horse brush and load it with medium ink. Add more brushwork to the body. The medium ink will run into the dark ink and create tones. Do not cover the whole body with ink: leave some blank spaces to create light effects.

STEP 4

Dry the small Mountain and Horse brush and load it with dark ink. Place the brush at a low angle along the side of the neck. Make a few side brushstrokes, using the press-and-lift technique, to create the mane. Press and lift away from the neck. Dry the brush and dip it into dark ink again. Place the tip of the brush at the rear end of the horse, where the tail is going to come. This time, hold the brush at a high angle to the paper, with the handle pointing in the direction in which the tail is flowing. Paint the tail with two or three brushstrokes, using the press-and-lift technique. In this illustration, I changed the direction of the tail to give a sense that it is swinging.

Step 1

Step 2

Step 3

Step 4

COLOURS
- Ink
- Burnt sienna
- Sap green

BRUSHES
- Red Bean brush
- No.3 Leopard and Wolf brush
- Small Orchid and Bamboo brush
- Small Mountain and Horse brush

PAINTING HORSES USING COLOURS

I am going to use colours to paint these horses. The illustration chiefly uses Method 2 (page 108), though I also used Method 1 (page 107). Refer to the section on combining methods of toning on page 111.

STEP 1

Draw an outline of the mare and foal, using diluted ink and the Red Bean brush. Next, prepare burnt sienna and diluted burnt sienna. Also prepare a darker burnt sienna by adding a tiny bit of ink to burnt sienna. Start with the mare. Use the No.3 Leopard and Wolf brush and clean water to wet the parts that you want to leave blank, such as the lower part of the neck and the top part of the hindquarters. Fully load the Small Orchid and Bamboo brush with the diluted burnt sienna and paint the parts, as in the illustration. Leave gaps between folds and the diluted burnt sienna so that later, when you apply the undiluted burnt sienna in the gaps, the darker colour will create shadows along the folds. I repeated the process with the foal, this time using the darkened burnt sienna.

STEP 2

While the diluted colours on the mare are still wet, fully load the small Mountain and Horse brush with the undiluted burnt sienna and finish applying colours to the mare. Next, dip the brush into the darkened burnt sienna and use it to enhance the shadows further. Leave all the brushwork to dry.

STEP 3

Dip a dry Red Bean brush into dark ink. Use broken lines to outline the horses. Next, load a dry small Mountain and Horse brush with dark ink. Holding the brush at a high angle to the paper, use the press-and-lift technique to paint the tails and the mane of the mare, and then use side brushstrokes, again made with the press-and-lift technique, to paint the mane of the foal. Dip a dry small Mountain and Horse brush into a mixture of sap green and burnt sienna. Press it on the mixing dish until the hairs separate and then paint grass with long dots.

Step 1

Step 2

Step 3

MORE ANIMALS PAINTED USING TONING TECHNIQUES

HORSE IN INK
This horse was painted in ink in the same way as the one on page 115.

YOUNG FOX
I used Methods 1 and 2 for this fox. I made a mixture of one part burnt sienna to one part cadmium orange for colouring, and two tones of the mixture and clean water for the toning. For the eyes, I used cadmium orange. I also highlighted the end of the tail and the cheeks with process white. You should use different brushes for different areas. For example, I used the Red Bean brush to paint the small details of the face and the Small Orchid and Bamboo brush and the No.3 Leopard and Wolf brush for the body.

BUFFALO IN INK
I used the same techniques to paint this buffalo.

GALLOPING HORSE
I mixed a reddish burnt sienna by adding a little alizarin crimson to burnt sienna. I diluted some of this mixture. I used the diluted reddish burnt sienna, the undiluted reddish burnt sienna, diluted ink and dark ink to paint this horse.

LIONESS DRINKING
I wanted to show you that you can create a range of colours for toning by mixing different amounts of two or three colours of your choice. For this illustration, I choose cadmium orange and burnt sienna. I then went on to mix them or dilute them, expanding the range of colours for painting.

I used three colours for the body: a mixture of two parts cadmium orange and one part burnt sienna, burnt sienna and a burnt sienna darkened with a little bit of ink. I then used the technique of toning with clean water, diluted cadmium mixture, cadmium mixture, burnt sienna and darkened burnt sienna.

PAINTING ELEPHANTS

COLOURS
- Ink
- Burnt sienna
- Process white
- Darkened burnt sienna, made by adding a tiny bit of ink to burnt sienna

BRUSHES
- Red Bean brush
- Small Mountain and Horse brush
- Large Bear-hair brush or Extra-large Mountain and Horse brush

I am painting African elephants in these illustrations. They are the largest land animals on earth, and there are many ways of painting them, most of which concentrate on the folds of the body. Elephants have many folds on their rough skin and here I have used the two-colour loading technique to express these folds. A good big brush, such as the large Bear-hair brush or the Extra-large Mountain and Horse brush, is useful for this purpose. Since I have used the large Bear-hair brush on a few occasions, I decided to use the Extra-large Mountain and Horse brush to paint all the following illustrations. It's worth noting that elephants are also frequently painted with two tones of ink.

The features of an elephant are comparatively more complex than those of other animals, so painting them is never easy. I shall start by showing you how to approach each part of the body. Finally, I shall put everything together.

Painting different parts of an elephant

The body has many folds. I am using the two-tone or two-colour technique to make the shady parts of the folds darker. Always make sure that the nib of the brush, bearing the darker tone or colour, is placed in the parts that are intended to be darker.

EARS

I always like to start with the ears, because these are a distinctive part of an elephant and reflect its character. Fully load the Extra-large Mountain and Horse brush with the darkened burnt sienna and dip the nib of the brush into ink. The ears of the elephant are naturally darker at the outer edges. Place the nib of the brush at the edge of the ear, holding the brush at a low angle to the paper. Paint a reverse fan brushstroke. Reload the brush with fresh colours and add another reverse fan brushstroke, next to the first one. Add successive brushstrokes until the whole ear is filled with colours. If your brush tip is not long enough to cover the whole ear, paint as near to the edge as you can first and then fill the rest of the ear with the darkened burnt sienna.

First reverse fan brushstroke

Completed ear

TRUNK

The tip of the trunk is usually darker. Fully load the Extra-large Mountain and Horse brush with darkened burnt sienna and dip the nib of the brush into dark ink. Holding the brush in a vertical position, place the nib of the brush at the tip of the trunk and shape it. Next, press the brush tip and continue to paint a long brushstroke along the trunk, pressing the brush to cover as much as possible of the area of the trunk. Clean the brush and reload with the darkened burnt sienna to touch up the rest of the trunk.

First brushstroke   Completed trunk

HEAD

After you have finished painting the ears and the trunk, you can fill in the parts of the rest of the head. Watch out for the areas that are in the shade. Fully load the Extra-large Mountain and Horse brush with the darkened burnt sienna and dip the nib of the brush into dark ink. Choose one part: for example, the cheek below the eyes and behind the ear. Place the nib of the brush in the shadowed area under the ears and use a reverse fan brushstroke to cover the area. Use a similar technique to paint the rest of the head.

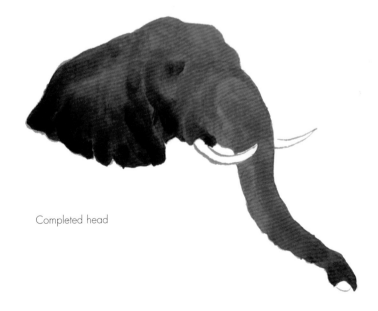

Completed head

LEGS

Fully load the Extra-large Mountain and Horse brush with the darkened burnt sienna and dip the nib of the brush into dark ink. Hold the brush in a vertical position. Use the nib of the brush to carefully paint around the toes. Press the brush and continue to move upwards along the leg, covering as much of the leg area as possible. Clean the brush and reload it with the darkened burnt sienna to touch up the remaining area of the leg.

First brushstroke

Completed leg

BODY

The body has many folds. We shall make use of the two-colour loading of the brush to paint these. Fully load the Extra-large Mountain and Horse brush with the darkened burnt sienna and dip the nib of the brush into dark ink. Hold the brush in an angle and place the nib of the brush at one end of a fold. Carefully move the brush along the fold with an extended long dot. Press the brush to fill the area of the fold. Reload the brush in the same manner and paint another fold. Continue to add more folds of skin in this way. For wider folds, you may have to hold the brush at a lower angle and use side brushstrokes to cover the area.

The first fold

Completing the body

ROUGH SKIN

Elephants have a lot of rough, folded skin. We can use a dry brush loaded with ink to paint this rough skin. Dip the small Mountain and Horse brush into medium ink. Wipe the brush on a piece of paper towel to remove excess moisture until it is dry. Holding the brush at a low angle on any part of the body where you want to show rough skin, rub the brush on the paper.

Rough skin

TAIL

The tail is insignificant in shape and size compared to the body, but if you are going to paint the back of an elephant and you want to show the tail, this is how you can do it. Load the brush with darkened burnt sienna and dip the nib of the brush into ink before painting the folds at the rear end, using the techniques already described. Next, colour the tail with the darkened burnt sienna and add the hair at the end of the tail with a little dark ink.

Elephant's tail

PAINTING AN ELEPHANT

Now we can put everything together and paint the elephant from start to finish.

STEP 1

Use the Red Bean brush to outline the elephant with diluted ink.

STEP 2

Prepare a mixture of burnt sienna darkened with a little ink. The elephant is a huge animal and when you apply colour to such a large area, the build-up of moisture in absorbent paper will cause the colour to run beyond the outlines you have sketched. For this reason, I start with colours. Apply these as described on pages 120–123. When all the colours have dried, I add outlines with dark ink. This way, you can correct any overrun of colours beyond the original outline. I always like to start with the fore parts and work my way backwards.

A tip about colouring: if you make the colour thicker and wipe the brush against the palette after loading it to squeeze out excessive moisture, this will minimize the chances of the colour running out of control.

STEP 3

Complete the colouring of the whole body.

STEP 4

Use a dry Red Bean brush and dark ink to draw lines wherever necessary. I added the outlines because I wanted to show you what they are like. You may choose to have a minimal number of outlines or none at all for your final artwork. A final step is to rub medium ink on the body with a dry small Mountain and Horse brush to make the skin rough. Use process white to colour the tusk. Dilute the dark ink and colour the toes.

Step 1

Step 2

Step 3

Step 4

PROJECT: KEEPING UP WITH MUM

COLOURS
- Ink
- Burnt sienna
- Process white
- Indigo
- Cobalt blue

BRUSHES
- Red Bean brush
- No.3 Leopard and Wolf brush
- Small Orchid and Bamboo brush
- Small Mountain and Horse brush
- Extra-large Mountain and Horse brush
- Hake brush

Any animal can be painted in more than one way. I have used a different approach to paint these elephants because I wanted to show you how you can be flexible when choosing methods to paint an animal.

STEP 1

Draw the outlines of the two elephants with the Red Bean brush and diluted ink.

STEP 2

Prepare burnt sienna, darkened with a little bit of ink. Use toning Methods 1 and 2 to apply colours to the elephants, first with clean water, then burnt sienna, then darkened burnt sienna, then diluted ink, finishing by applying dark ink to different parts of the elephants. Use different sizes of brush for different parts of the body: No.3 Leopard and Wolf brush and the Small Orchid and Bamboo brush for smaller areas, and the small Mountain and Horse brush and Extra-large Mountain and Horse brush for the larger areas. Do not paint the feet completely: leave some parts unfinished to create the effect of dust raised by the running elephants. Leave all colours to dry.

STEP 3

When all brushwork areas are dry, use the Red Bean brush and dark ink to add outlines, eyes, toes and folds on the ears, trunks and bodies. Dip the small Mountain and Horse brush into medium ink. Wipe the brush on a paper towel to remove excess moisture. Rub the brush on the body of the mother elephant to make it look rough. Load the small Mountain and Horse brush with dark ink and add brushwork to the ground, using a mixture of lines with the press-and-lift technique and side brushstrokes.

STEP 4

Prepare indigo, diluted indigo, cobalt blue, diluted cobalt blue, burnt sienna and diluted burnt sienna. Wet the area you want to leave blank with clean water, using the Small Orchid and Bamboo brush. Next, use a mixture of the colours you prepared to apply washes to the sky and the ground. You can use a small Mountain and Horse brush, the Extra-large Mountain and Horse brush, the Hake brush or a mixture of all three.

USING BROKEN BRUSHSTROKES

For a broken brushstroke, press the brush tip until the hairs separate before or after loading it with colour. A brushstroke made with this brush will leave blank gaps. In animal painting, broken brushstrokes are popularly used for creating hair or fur and in this session we shall explore the range of broken brushstrokes that can be created with Chinese brushes.

Different animals have different types of hair. For example, squirrels have fluffy hair in their tails, but the hairs in their bodies are closely packed. Badger hairs are coarse and create wave-like shadings in the body. The hedgehog's bristles are very coarse and have white tips. These varying effects can be achieved by using a wide range of brushes and loading them with differing amounts of colour. Three different brushes have been used in this session to create broken brushstrokes: a small Landscape brush, a large Landscape brush and a small Mountain and Horse brush. Broken brushstrokes created by each of these brushes vary in size and texture. In order for the broken brushstrokes to be effective, the following three practices are essential.

BEFORE MAKING BROKEN BRUSHSTROKES

1   Make sure the brush is dry before loading it with colour. In this way you can control the amount of moisture you are going to load on to your brush. If your brush is wet, this will cause the colours to run and destroy the effect of broken brushstrokes, so wipe it thoroughly dry with a towel or paper towel before loading it with colour.

2   Make the colour thick for the broken brushstrokes. Too watery a colour will result in the colour running on the absorbent paper, destroying the effect of the broken brushstrokes. I mix one part of colour from the tube with, at most, two parts of water. You can experiment with different amounts of water to discover the mix you are happy with. If you are preparing ink by grinding the ink stick, make the ink thick. If you are using liquid ink, leave the ink in the open for about ten minutes so that it thickens up before use.

3   After the brush is loaded with colour, press the end on the palette to separate the hairs. Do not press it on the absorbent paper because the paper will absorb the moisture, destroying the delicate balance and ruining the final effect. After one or two brushstrokes, the hairs may come back together as it is the nature of brush hairs to return to a point. If this happens, press the brush tip again to separate the hairs.

Before showing you all the different brushstrokes, let's take a little time to understand the brushes we are using in this chapter: the small Landscape brush, the large Landscape brush and the small Mountain and Horse brush. Wolf hairs are softer and finer than horsehair, so wolf-hair brushes make broken brushstrokes with finer lines, creating a softer effect, while horsehair brushes make brushstrokes with thicker and harder lines.

The width of a broken brushstroke will depend on the size of the brush tip. The small Landscape brush has the smallest brush tip of the three, so a broken brushstroke produced by this brush is narrow, while one made by the small Mountain and Horse brush will be wider. The length of a brushstroke will also depend on the size of the brush tip. For example, the small Landscape brush can only hold sufficient moisture to sustain a short brushstroke, while the small Mountain and Horse brush is able to make a longer brushstroke. So if you are not using the three brushes specified here and want to choose your own brushes for painting broken brushstrokes, do bear these characteristics in mind when you are buying your brushes.

You can create many types of broken brushstroke with these three brushes. I am going to show you four types here.

Technique 1
Broken brushstrokes with separated lines

Technique 3
Coarse broken brushstrokes

Technique 2
Denser broken brushstrokes with lines

Technique 4
Closely packed brushstrokes

I shall be demonstrating each technique and illustrating it with animal paintings.

In this session, if the bodies of the animals are coloured with toning techniques, I have normally used the technique for applying colours separately. Just to remind you: I start with clean water at one edge and then apply the lighter colour up to the edge of the clean water, finishing with the darker colour next to the light colour.

TECHNIQUE 1: BROKEN BRUSHSTROKES WITH SEPARATED LINES

Dip a dry brush tip halfway into ink. Press the brush on the palette until the hairs separate. Holding the brush in a vertical position, paint a long brushstroke. The resulting brushstroke has uniform thin separated lines.

Broken brushstrokes made with the small Landscape brush are narrow, short and soft. Those made by the large Landscape brush are wider, longer and soft. The strokes made by the small Mountain and Horse brush are wide, long and hard (see overleaf).

Use different brushes to create different areas of hair. For example, the hairs of the face and head of an animal are shorter and finer, so the small Landscape brush is more suitable for this purpose. Many animals have soft, short hairs on their bodies. A large Landscape brush will be good for this. The male lion has long hairs in his mane, for which the small Mountain and Horse brush is a perfect tool (see page 134).

Broken brushstrokes made with the
small Landscape brush are narrow,
short and soft.

Straight brushstroke

Curved brushstroke

Press-and-lift brushstroke

Broken brushstrokes made with the
large Landscape brush are wider,
longer and soft.

Straight brushstroke

Curved brushstroke

Press-and-lift brushstroke

Broken brushstrokes made with the small
Mountain and Horse brush are wide, long
and hard.

Straight brushstroke

Curved brushstroke

Press-and-lift brushstroke

TECHNIQUE 2: DENSER BROKEN BRUSHSTROKES WITH LINES

If you repeatedly apply Technique 1 to the same surface, the final brushwork will be dense because the more brushstrokes you add, the denser the hair. You can make use of different degrees of density to control the shading of an animal's body: the denser the brushstrokes, the darker the hair.

USING THE SMALL LANDSCAPE BRUSH

Here, the brushwork is lighter ———

——— Here, the brushwork is darker

Brushwork created with Technique 1

Brushwork created with Technique 2

USING THE LARGE LANDSCAPE BRUSH

Here, the brushwork is lighter ———

——— Here, the brushwork is darker

Brushwork created with Technique 1

Brushwork created with Technique 2

USING THE SMALL MOUNTAIN AND HORSE BRUSH

Here, the brushwork is lighter ———

——— Here, the brushwork is darker

Brushwork created with Technique 1

Brushwork created with Technique 2

TECHNIQUE 3: COARSE BROKEN BRUSHSTROKES

Fully load a dry brush with colour or ink and press the brush against the side of the palette to remove as much moisture as possible. The brush should be wetter than the one used in Technique 1. After loading, press the brush tip on the palette until the hairs separate. Hold the brush in a vertical position and paint a broken brushstroke. The lines of the resulting brushstroke are thicker and closer together than those made with Technique 1, so the hairs created with this technique are coarser.

Coarse broken brushstrokes, made with the small Landscape brush.

Coarse broken brushstrokes, made with the large Landscape brush.

Coarse broken brushstrokes, made with the small Mountain and Horse brush.

TECHNIQUE 4: CLOSELY PACKED BRUSHSTROKES

Fully load a dry brush with thick colour. Press the brush on the palette until the hairs separate. Hold the brush in a vertical position and paint a brushstroke. The lines will be even thicker and only the starting point of the brushstroke will have a broken effect. The rest will be solid. This is especially useful for painting animals with closely packed hairs in the body and only a few loose hairs at the edges (see the otter on page 140).

Broken brushstrokes, made using Technique 4 with the small Landscape brush.

Broken brushstrokes, made using Technique 4 with the large Landscape brush.

Broken brushstrokes, made using Technique 4 with the small Mountain and Horse brush.

COLOURS
- Ink
- Burnt sienna
- Permanent rose
- Cadmium orange
- Gamboge
- Process white

BRUSHES
- Red Bean brush
- Outline brush
- Small Mountain and Horse brush
- Small Landscape brush
- Small Orchid and Bamboo brush
- No.3 Leopard and Wolf brush
- No.1 Wolf-hair brush for Painting

LION

This painting uses Technique 1, broken brushstrokes with separated lines (see page 129). The lion's mane has layers of different lengths of long hair. I began building up the framework with a dry brush and dark ink. I then used colours to build up the different tones and at the same time make the mane thick and lush.

Step 1

STEP 1

Use the Red Bean brush and diluted ink to sketch the head of a lion.

STEP 2

Use the Outline brush to draw the face of the lion with dark ink. You can use the cushion technique to help steady the hand holding the brush (see page 45). Dip the brush tip of a small dry Mountain and Horse brush halfway into dark ink. Press the brush tip on the palette until the hairs separate. Paint with long brushstrokes to create the mane, following the pattern of your original outline. Use a mixture of straight, curved and press-and-lift broken brushstrokes. Use the same technique to add some texture to the face with the small Landscape brush. Leave all ink brushwork to dry completely before adding colours.

Step 2

STEP 3

Prepare a mixture of one part burnt sienna and one part cadmium orange. Make the colour thick, adding, at most, two equal parts of water to the colours. Use the same technique as in Step 2 to colour the mane with the small Mountain and Horse brush and then use medium ink to create shades in the mane with the Small Orchid and Bamboo brush. Paint the face with diluted ink and burnt sienna, using the No.3 Leopard and Wolf brush and leaving out the hairs under the eyes and chin.

STEP 4

Use permanent rose to paint the nose. Colour the eyes with burnt sienna around the pupils and the rest of the eyes with gamboge. You can use the Red Bean brush for colouring both the nose and the eyes. Add a few more whiskers with process white, using the No.1 Wolf-hair brush for Painting. If your colours have run into the parts that are supposed to be left blank, such as the parts under the eye or under the chin, you can cover the overrun parts with process white to restore them.

Steps 3 and 4

COLOURS
- Ink
- Burnt sienna
- Permanent rose
- Sap green

BRUSHES
- Red Bean brush
- Outline brush
- Small Mountain and Horse brush
- Large Landscape brush
- Small Landscape brush
- No.3 Leopard and Wolf brush
- Small Orchid and Bamboo brush
- No.1 Wolf-hair brush for Painting

SQUIRREL

We are going to paint a grey squirrel, this time combining Technique 1 with Technique 2 (pages 129–131). To do this, we shall use all three brushes: the small Landscape brush, the large Landscape brush and the small Mountain and Horse brush.

STEP 1

Use the Red Bean brush and diluted ink to outline the squirrel.

STEP 2

We shall use dark ink to paint all the ink brushwork before applying the colours. Use the Outline brush to draw the details, such as the eyes, nose, ears and feet. Use the small Mountain and Horse brush to paint the tail of the squirrel with broken brushstrokes, using Technique 1. Next, use the large Landscape brush to apply broken brushstrokes to the body. Create shading by applying more brushstrokes to the darker areas. Finally, use the small Landscape brush to add shorter broken brushstrokes to the face. Leave all ink brushwork to dry.

STEP 3

Use a toning technique to apply colours. Prepare two colours: burnt sienna and a burnt sienna darkened with a little ink. Apply the colours with the No.3 Leopard and Wolf brush or the Small Orchid and Bamboo brush, depending on the size of the squirrel. You can actually use both brushes: one loaded with burnt sienna and one loaded with the darkened burnt sienna. Begin by applying clean water along the edge of the parts which are to be blank, then add burnt sienna to the edge of the clean water, followed by the darkened burnt sienna. Apply diluted permanent rose to the inside of the ears with the Red Bean brush. Using the No.1 Wolf-hair brush for Painting, dot the pupil of the eye with process white. Use the Red Bean brush to colour the apple with sap green and diluted permanent rose. Finally, paint the tufts of grass in sap green and ink, using short broken brushstrokes.

Step 1

Step 2

Step 3

BADGER

COLOURS
• Ink
• Burnt sienna
• Process white

BRUSHES
• Red Bean brush
• Outline brush
• Small Landscape brush
• Large Landscape brush
• Small Mountain and Horse brush
• No.3 Leopard and Wolf brush
• Small Orchid and Bamboo brush
• No.1 Wolf-hair brush for Painting

The badger has coarse hair on its body, the hairs forming waves like shading. I use Technique 3, coarse broken brushstrokes, for this (see page 132) with Technique 1, broken brushstrokes with separated lines (see page 129), for the tail.

STEP 1
Use the Red Bean brush to outline a badger with diluted ink. A badger has definite white patches on its head and neck. Mark these parts so that they can be left blank when colour is applied.

STEP 2
Use the Outline brush and dark ink to draw the face and the feet of the badger. I used the small Landscape brush to paint broken brushstrokes with Technique 3 for the head and the small Mountain and Horse brush for the body. For the tail, I used the large Landscape brush and Technique 1. Leave the ink to dry.

STEP 3
Prepare burnt sienna and burnt sienna darkened with a tiny bit of ink. Use a toning technique to colour the body. Begin by applying clean water with the No.3 Leopard and Wolf brush to the parts that will stay blank, such as the lower abdomen and part of the face. Next, use the Small Orchid and Bamboo brush to apply burnt sienna up to the edge of the clean water. Finally, add the darkened burnt sienna. Also using the darkened burnt sienna, colour the nose and feet. Dip the No.1 Wolf-hair brush for Painting into process white and paint a tiny dot in the centre of each eye. See how this brings the badger to life.

Step 1

Step 2

Step 3

OTTER

COLOURS
- Ink
- Burnt sienna
- Process white
- Indigo

BRUSHES
- Red Bean brush
- Outline brush
- Large Landscape brush
- Small Landscape brush
- No.3 Leopard and Wolf brush
- No.1 Wolf-hair brush for Painting
- Small Mountain and Horse brush

The hairs of an otter are tightly packed. We shall use Technique 4, closely packed brushstrokes (see page 133) to paint the hairs, which are wet all the time and therefore reflect the light. We can use process white for this effect.

STEP 1

Use the Red Bean brush and diluted ink to sketch the outline of an otter. Use the Outline brush and dark ink to go over some of the features, as shown in the illustration.

STEP 2

Prepare burnt sienna and burnt sienna darkened with a little ink. Use the Red Bean brush to paint the tips of the toes with burnt sienna. Before the colour dries, add the darkened burnt sienna and extend the colouring into the legs. Paint the body with the large Landscape brush and the face with the small Landscape brush, using Technique 4 and the darkened burnt sienna. When you are painting the parts that have loose hair – for example, the parts next to the tummy, around the face and part of the tail – make sure that you place the tip of the brush, which has the separated hairs, on the outer edge. Add the darkened burnt sienna to the webs of the feet.

STEP 3

Dip the No.3 Leopard and Wolf brush into diluted burnt sienna. Colour the face and neck. When you are painting the neck, apply clean water first and then diluted burnt sienna next to it, to create toning. Use the No.1 Wolf-hair brush for Painting to highlight the hair with process white. Make sure you follow the contour of the body. Finally, paint a dot of process white on each eye. Dip the small Mountain and Horse brush into diluted indigo and sweep on a few lines to represent the water current.

Step 1

Step 2

Step 3

MORE ANIMALS PAINTED WITH BROKEN BRUSHSTROKES

BORNEO ORANG-UTAN

An orang-utan has different lengths of hair on different parts of the body, those on the head being longer. I used the small Mountain and Horse brush to start painting the hair with ink using Technique 1 (see page 129). Next, I made a mixture of two parts burnt sienna and one part cadmium red deep and used this to add colour to the hairs. I made another mixture with three parts burnt sienna to one part cadmium red deep. I diluted this and used it, together with diluted ink, to colour the body and the face. I used the Small Orchid and Bamboo brush for colouring, wetting the lower edge of the shoulder with clean water before applying the colour. This caused the colour to run into the wet area and create a toning effect.

I coloured the lips and nose with diluted permanent rose, using the Red Bean brush. The edges of the lips are left blank because the Borneo orang-utans have discoloured edges to their lips, caused by the highly acidic content of their favourite fruits, which are those of the rengas tree.

LONG-HAIRED CAT

Though the hairs of these cats are considered to be long, they are still short compared with those of lions and orang-utans. As the hairs form short waves, I used the small Landscape brush to paint them, mostly with curved broken brushstrokes using Technique 1. I used a little diluted burnt sienna and diluted ink to add shading to the hairs. I did not use much colour because I wanted you to be able to see the ink brushwork making up the hairs. I used cadmium orange to colour the eyes, with permanent rose for the nose. I shaded the outer edges of the eyes with diluted ink before applying the colour.

RED SQUIRREL
I used burnt sienna, tinted with a little alizarin crimson, for the colour of the red squirrel.

GREY SQUIRREL EATING A NUT
See how you can achieve the soft effect of the tail by using broken brushstrokes as I did on this grey squirrel.

A VISITOR TO MY GARDEN
I always leave a saucer of milk in my garden to attract small animals. I found this badger one night hungrily lapping up my offering. I used the technique described on page 138 to paint it.

HUNGRY RACCOON

The raccoon has a distinctive facial pattern of white and black. The fur of the raccoon is coarse, being similar to that of the badger. The procedure for painting a raccoon is also similar to that used for a badger. Using Technique 3, I started the body with all the ink brushstrokes. When all the ink was dry, I used burnt sienna and a darkened burnt sienna to add colours.

HEDGEHOG

The bristles of a hedgehog are very tough and spiky. These were created using the large Landscape brush and Technique 4. I used a mixture of burnt sienna and darkened burnt sienna for the colours. When the colours were dry, I used the No.1 Wolf-hair brush for Painting to add the short lines on the body, first with dark ink and then with process white.

OTTER MUM AND PUP

An otter mum is very protective of her pup. She wraps her long tail around it and is always on the lookout for any predators. Use the same instructions as for painting the otter on page 140 to paint this pair. I used a lighter burnt sienna for the pup against the darker colour of the mum.

PROJECT: A POLAR BEAR

COLOURS
- Ink
- Burnt sienna
- Process white
- Indigo (optional)
- Cobalt blue (optional)

BRUSHES
- Red Bean brush
- No.3 Leopard and Wolf brush
- Small Landscape brush
- Large Landscape brush
- Outline brush
- Small Mountain and Horse brush

Painting animals with white hair requires extra work. First, you need a darker background to show off the white colour of the animal, so we shall start by applying a colour wash to a piece of absorbent Xuan paper. Please refer to the Appendix (page 172) for instructions on applying washes to absorbent Xuan paper. This can be a plain or multi-coloured wash. In this project, I began by applying a plain wash to the paper, using a mixture of one part indigo to one part cobalt blue. Next, I added some patches of very dilute burnt sienna. Alternatively, you can use a piece of ready-tinted absorbent Xuan paper. This is usually available in the art shops where you get your Chinese painting materials. You do not necessarily have to choose a blue background.

STEP 1
Use the Red Bean brush to sketch the outline of the polar bear and the rocks on a coloured absorbent Xuan paper. You can sketch with diluted ink or diluted process white.

STEP 2
Add some shading with diluted burnt sienna and diluted ink to those parts of the body of the bear that are in shadow, such as between the legs and the divisions of the paws.

STEP 3
Dilute process white by mixing one part process white with one part of water. Apply this process white to the polar bear with the No.3 Leopard and Wolf brush. Leave the colour to dry. This will form the background colour of the body of the bear, making it easier for you to paint the broken brushstrokes. If you paint process white on absorbent Xuan paper, the colour usually causes the Xuan paper to stick to the paper underneath. If you lift the painting paper when this happens, you may tear it. To avoid this, lay your Xuan paper on a piece of paper towel when you are applying process white, as paper towel has an uneven pattern that prevents the Xuan paper sticking to it.

STEP 4
Paint the bear with process white, using a combination of Technique 1 and Technique 2 (pages 129–131). Use the small and large Landscape brushes.

STEP 5
Use the Outline brush to paint the small details on the face and the feet with dark ink. Fully load the small Mountain and Horse brush with process white. Paint multiple side brushstrokes with press and lift to make up the icy rocks.

PAINTING ANIMALS WITH PATTERNS

Many animals have beautiful and striking patterns on their bodies. In order to make painting patterns more effective in non-outline painting, we have developed the Dry Method and the Wet Method, each of which has variations. The finished effects of each method are very different, so you can choose whichever suits your concept of your chosen animal.

In this session, I have used a mixture of different toning techniques to apply the skin colours to the animals.

DRY METHODS

To paint an animal with patterns, you need to paint the patterns as well as applying the skin colours to the body. In the dry method, you can start either with the patterns or with the colours, provided the first is dry before you start the other. Patterns created using dry methods are sharper and are therefore suitable for painting predators, as the sharper images created by the patterns make them look more powerful and aggressive.

DRY METHOD 1

Draw the patterns with dark ink first. The size of brush used will depend on the size of the patterns. For an animal such as a tiger, I use the Red Bean brush for the face. For the body, you could use either the No.3 Leopard and Wolf brush or the small Landscape brush to paint the smaller brushwork, and the large Landscape brush or the small Mountain and Horse brush to paint the large brushwork. Skin colours will be added after the ink is dry.

DRY METHOD 2

Begin with the skin colour. I let the colours dry before adding the patterns. Refer to Dry Method 1 for suggestions about which brushes to use.

An example made with Dry Method 1

An example made with Dry Method 2

WET METHODS

When using wet methods, you can also start with either the skin colours or the patterns. If you start with colours, you must add the patterns while the colours are still wet. Similarly, if you start with the patterns, you must apply the colours while the patterns are still wet. Either way, this will make the patterns run, creating a soft and fluffy effect. This method is therefore more suitable for smaller animals.

WET METHOD 1

Start with the skin colours; it is better for the applied colours to settle and dry a little bit before patterns are added. The patterns will still run as long as the surface is damp, but they will tend to run out of control if the surface is too wet.

In the illustration below, I began by applying burnt sienna to the paper. I let the colour settle a little bit and then added the patterns with dark ink. Refer to Dry Method 1 for suggestions about which brushes to use.

WET METHOD 2

Start by painting the patterns. While the patterns are still wet, apply the skin colours on top. The colours also run, but the effect is not as soft as with Wet Method 1.

An example made with
Wet Method 1

An example made with
Wet Method 2

COLOURS
- Ink
- Cadmium orange
- Burnt sienna
- Sap green
- Permanent rose

BRUSHES
- Red Bean brush
- Outline brush
- No.3 Leopard and Wolf brush
- Small Orchid and Bamboo brush
- Small Mountain and Horse brush

PAINTING TIGERS

Tigers are famous for their beautiful velvety skin with striking dark markings. Their faces are also very distinctive, with clear, dark patterns. They can be very aggressive, yet when they are relaxed, they can look very tame and approachable.

I used Dry Method 1 (page 148) to paint the patterns of this leaping tiger. Though many artists favour the wet method for its fluffy effect, I personally prefer the sharper effect created by the dry methods.

STEP 1
Use the Red Bean brush and diluted ink to sketch the tiger. Take care when you draw the face because the features are very unusual and show the character of the tiger.

STEP 2
Use dark ink to draw the face. You can use either the Outline brush or the Red Bean brush. I used both: the Outline brush to draw some of the fine lines and the Red Bean brush for the rest of the brushwork. Vary the thickness of the lines by pressing and lifting the brush. Using the Red Bean brush, draw the outline of the body with dark ink. Next, dip the No.3 Leopard and Wolf brush into the dark ink and add the patterns on the body. Press the brush for the wider brushstrokes and lift it for thinner lines. For even wider lines, use the small Mountain and Horse brush. Let all the brushwork dry before the next step.

STEP 3
Prepare burnt sienna and a mixture of two parts cadmium orange to one part burnt sienna. Do not make the colours too watery: you need a thick colour to create the thick, rich and velvety quality of the fur. I used three colours for toning: clean water, the prepared mixture and burnt sienna. Using the No.3 Leopard and Wolf brush, apply clean water to the chest, rear end, lower abdomen, part of the legs and the feet. Refer to the illustration to see which parts are to be left blank. Fully load the Small Orchid and Bamboo brush with the cadmium orange mixture and apply it to the body, overlapping the edges of the clean water a little. The colour will start to run into the water.

STEP 4
Finally, use the small Mountain and Horse brush to apply burnt sienna to the body. This will create the toning effect formed by the three colours. Also apply burnt sienna to the face. Use the Red Bean brush to colour the eyes with sap green and the nose and tongue with permanent rose.

Step 1

Step 2

Step 3

Step 4

PAINTING LEOPARDS

Leopards display distinctive and beautiful patterns, which are usually made up of rosettes and dots. I used Dry Method 1 (page 148) to paint the patterns. Dot the centres of the rosettes with burnt sienna before applying colour to the body. The three colours creating the tones are clean water, a mixture of three parts gamboge to one part burnt sienna, and a mixture of equal amounts of gamboge and burnt sienna.

STROLLING LEOPARD
A leopard always takes a slow approach, eyeing its prey before eventually leaping into fast action.

PAINTING JAGUARS

Leopards and jaguars are similar, but the latter are bigger and their bodies are sturdier, whereas leopards are smaller, more streamlined and thinner. The markings on both animals are also similar, but the rosettes of leopards are smaller than those of the jaguar. Another difference is that there are dots in the centres of the rosettes of jaguars, but not in those of the leopards. To paint the jaguar shown opposite (top), I used the same techniques and colours that I used for the leopard. For the grass, I used a dry small Mountain and Horse brush to paint long dots of sap green.

JAGUAR FOLLOWING A SCENT
It looks as if this jaguar is on to something.

Rosette patterns of jaguars

PAINTING CHEETAHS

Again, we can use the techniques described above to paint cheetahs. The bodies of cheetahs are marked with dots of different sizes. For the colour of the body, mix equal amounts of yellow ochre and burnt sienna. Dilute a small amount of this mixture with water and then use clean water, the diluted mixture and the undiluted mixture to create the tones. Colour the tongue with permanent rose.

CHEETAH STRETCHING
Yawn – that's enough for today!

PAINTING GIRAFFES

Giraffes also have very distinctive patterns on their bodies. These usually consist of patches that look like geometric figures. The colours of the patches vary, depending on where the animals originally come from: some are darker in colour, while others are lighter; some have dark areas in the middle of the patches and others don't. Adults are darker in colour than their young. In this illustration, I added a little bit of ink into burnt sienna to make the colour darker. I used this darkened burnt sienna to paint the mother and burnt sienna for the calf. I wanted to show you their faces, so I did not include the whole of their bodies: they are simply too tall.

PAINTING ZEBRAS

I am always amazed by the patterning on the body of a zebra, formed by dark lines alternating with lines of lighter colour. The lines extend to the mane and the tail and almost appear like a painted artwork. We can draw a zebra with dark ink and diluted ink. Every line on the body is different and each one curves according to the contour of the body. Use the press-and-lift technique to achieve the different widths of the lines. As for brushes, use the Outline brush and the Red Bean brush to draw the lines on the face, and the small Landscape brush and the large Landscape brush for those on the body. Let all the ink dry. With the No.3 Leopard and Wolf brush, use a diluted burnt sienna to create shaded areas and then use the diluted burnt sienna to retrace the diluted ink lines with the Red Bean brush.

A UNIQUE PATTERN
No two zebras have the same arrangement of lines on their bodies. The individual pattern of a zebra's markings is like its signature.

MOTHER AND CALF
This young giraffe is painted in burnt sienna while the mother's colouring is made up of different tones of darkened burnt sienna.

PAINTING CATS

COLOURS
• Ink
• Burnt sienna
• Alizarin crimson
• Sap green
• Permanent rose

BRUSHES
• Red Bean brush
• Outline brush
• No.3 Leopard and
  Wolf brush
• Small Orchid and
  Bamboo brush

The patterns on cats are soft, so the wet methods of adding pattern (see page 149) are ideal for this purpose.

STEP 1

If you are using liquid ink, pour it out and leave it to thicken up. If you are using ink made by grinding an ink stick, thicken it with a bit more grinding. Start by using the Red Bean brush to make a sketch in diluted ink.

STEP 2

Use the Outline brush and dark ink to draw the face, ears, paws and lower abdomen.

STEP 3

Apply colours to the body. I mixed a little bit of alizarin crimson into burnt sienna. I then darkened a small amount of the colour with a tiny bit of ink and used it for shading. Using clean water and the No.3 Leopard and Wolf brush, start by wetting the areas where you want to have the lightest tone (or leave it blank): the front, lower part of the legs and part of the face. Apply the mixture, overlapping a little bit of the clean water patch with the Small Orchid and Bamboo brush, and then add shading with the darkened mixture.

STEP 4

While the colour is still wet, dip the No.3 Leopard and Wolf brush into the dark, thick ink and draw the pattern. Paint the nose with permanent rose and the eyes with sap green, using the Red Bean brush.

Step 1

Step 2

Step 3

Step 4

MORE CATS

A GINGER CAT

I mixed one part of burnt sienna with one part of cadmium orange.
I then diluted some of this mixture to create a light tone. I used these
two tones to paint the body of the cat. The pattern was applied with
burnt sienna. I used permanent rose to paint the nose and a mixture
of one part sap green to one part gamboge for the eye.

GOT YOU – ALMOST
First of all, I prepared diluted burnt sienna and diluted burnt sienna, darkened with ink. I used these two diluted colours for the body. Next, I applied the pattern with dark, thick ink. I used gamboge for the eyes and permanent rose for the nose.

LESSER PANDA OR FIRE CAT
The lesser panda is also commonly known as the red panda or fire cat, because of the reddish colour of its fur. The front of the body, however, is black. Its face is a beautiful pattern of reddish brown and white patches. The body is made up of shades of brown and reddish brown. The tail has stripes of two tones of the reddish brown. I used a mixture of two parts burnt sienna to one part alizarin crimson for the reddish brown. I also prepared a diluted burnt sienna for toning. I used the wet method to create the patterns of the tail: first I applied a diluted reddish brown with a side brushstroke to form the shape of the tail and then I added the ring pattern with the undiluted reddish brown. I painted the body by applying alternate stripes of diluted burnt sienna and the undiluted reddish-brown colour.

PROJECT: A STROLL IN THE SNOW

COLOURS
- Ink
- Cadmium orange
- Burnt sienna
- Sap green
- Permanent rose
- Indigo
- Cobalt blue

BRUSHES
- Red Bean brush
- Outline brush
- Small Landscape brush
- No.3 Leopard and Wolf brush
- Small Orchid and Bamboo brush
- Small Mountain and Horse brush
- Hake brush, 5 cm (2 in) wide

We are now going to paint this snowy scene with two tigers.

STEP 1

Use the Red Bean brush and diluted ink to draw a sketch of the tigers and the pine trees.

STEP 2

Draw the faces of the tigers with dark ink, using the Outline brush. Use the Red Bean brush and the small Landscape brush to add all the other features that should be in dark ink, such as the outlines of the ears and strong legs.

STEP 3

Prepare a mixture of two parts of cadmium orange to one part burnt sienna. Use the No.3 Leopard and Wolf brush to wet the parts you want to leave blank – the lower abdomen, the feet and part of the faces – with clean water. Dry the brush before dipping it into the mixture and adding colours next to the clean-water areas, overlapping these a little. Next, use the Small Orchid and Bamboo brush to apply burnt sienna to finish colouring. Paint the eyes with sap green, using the Red Bean brush. Paint the tongues and the noses with permanent rose, again using the Red Bean brush.

STEP 4

Make a dark green by adding a little bit of indigo to sap green. Draw the pine trees with dark ink, using the Red Bean brush. Use short lines to paint the pine needles. Dip the No.3 Leopard and Wolf brush into the dark green mixture and add the colours to the trees.

STEP 5

Prepare a mixture of one part cobalt blue to one part indigo. Dilute part of this mixture. Dip the small Mountain and Horse brush into the diluted mixture. Wipe the brush on a piece of paper towel to make the brush dry. Hold the brush in a vertical position and sweep a few dry brushstrokes across the paper to create the mountain slopes.

STEP 6

Use the hake brush and the two tones of the blue mixture to add washes around the pine trees. First, apply the diluted tone to the edges around the trees. Next, load the No.3 Leopard and Wolf brush with the undiluted tone and carefully fill up the background of the trees. When you colour in the spaces between the pine leaves, leave blank spaces above the leaves to create the impression of snow on top of the leaves.

4 ANIMAL GALLERY

PANDAS – MUM AND CUB
This is just a matter of simple brushstrokes. The beauty of painting pandas is their simplicity.

BADGERS' COMFORT

For this painting, I used sweeping brushstrokes more
expressively than for the badger on page 139, and
created the fur with the help of process white rather
than leaving spaces.

RUN, RUN
The techniques used for this composition are very simple: press-and-lift, dry brushwork and washes, with only ink and burnt sienna. The variation of the basic techniques and the range of tones used bring everything to life.

GOING AFTER PREY
A multi-colour wash, the droplets of process white and the swinging tail bring this tiger into action.

A SPRING ROMANCE BLOSSOMING

To create atmosphere in your work, elements other than
the animals themselves are important. Here the informal
dotting of the blossoms and the background give a sense
of spring and romance.

SWEET DREAM
By now, you should be able to recognize the sweeping brushstrokes forming the tail, limbs and back. Controlled sweeping brushstrokes need not be messy, even with two-tone or two-colour loading.

KILLER WHALE

A killer whale, with its simple patches of black and white, is a very striking and beautiful animal. Adding the water with dry brushwork and washes makes the whale emerging from the water even more dramatic.

RAIN, RAIN, GO AWAY!

Gorillas do not seek shelter when it rains: they sit through it. Wet and dry techniques combine very well to create this artwork. The rule is: don't hesitate; feel free!

READY FOR THE KILL

The sweeping brushstroke is a very effective tool for painting animals in action.

HORSES

It is really fun sketching horses and dotting colours liberally. Once you have mastered your techniques, you will be able to draw lines, execute brushstrokes and dot colours with great freedom. As my master once said, 'The brush becomes an extension of your hand and your hand an extension of your heart.' You can say freely what you want to say from your heart with a Chinese brush. Try it!

APPENDIX

WASHES

Tinting a Xuan paper

If you want to tint a piece of absorbent Xuan paper, you will need a Hake brush at least 5 cm (2 in) wide. It is easier to apply a wash to Xuan paper with diluted colours, as thick colour forms hard lines on absorbent paper. If you want the colour to be darker, apply a first wash of diluted colour and then, while the wash is still wet, add a wash of thicker colour. The initial wash allows the second one to diffuse instead of forming hard lines.

Applying the first strip of colour

The most practical way to tint a piece of Xuan paper is to lay your paper on a flat surface over a piece of clean newsprint. Fully load your Hake brush with the diluted colour and start with your brush at the top of one corner. Touch your brush lightly on the paper and move across the top to form a strip. Do not press too hard on the paper or you will create creases. Reload your brush and add another strip, overlapping the first one a little bit. Always move your brush in the same direction – adding strips in the opposite direction will also create creases. Add successive strips until you have finished applying colour to the entire piece of paper.

Place another piece of dry, clean newsprint on top of the wet Xuan paper. Turn over the whole pile – newsprint, Xuan paper and clean newsprint. The second clean sheet of newsprint is now under the Xuan paper. Peel off the original newsprint sheet and leave the Xuan paper to dry.

Multiple-colour tinting

If you want to tint a piece of absorbent Xuan paper with more than one colour, it is always advisable to start by wetting the paper with diluted tones of the various colours. While these are still wet, you can add stronger tones to build up the intensity of the colours until the desired tones are reached.

Partial washes

You can apply colours to just one area of your paper, as I have done in many of my artworks. You can use a Hake brush, or select a large brush such as the Extra-large Mountain and Horse brush, the large Bear-hair brush, a Ti brush or a Dou brush to apply the wash with side brushstrokes.

If you want to give softer edges to your partial wash, apply clean water along the edge of the area for the wash before applying colour. This will help the colour to diffuse softly.

Tinting with multiple colours

Partial wash

Partial wash with soft edges

SUPPLIERS

US

EChinaArt Store
Tel: 1-718-938-6588
www.echinaart.com

China Art Material and Art Books
China Cultural Centre
970 North Broadway
Suite 210
Los Angeles
CA 90012
USA
Tel: 1-213-626-7295
www.ocac.gov.tw

OAS (Oriental Art Supply)
21522 Surveyor Circle
Huntington Beach
CA 92646
USA
Tel: 1-714-969-4470
Tel: 1-800-969-4471
www.orientalartsupply.com

**Oriental Culture Enterprises
Co., Inc.**
13–17 Elizabeth Street
2nd Floor
NY 10013
USA
Tel: 1-212-226-8461
www.oceweb.com/en/

Rochester Art Supply
150 West Main Street
Rochester
NY 14614
USA
Tel: 1-585-546-6509
www. fineartstore.com

UK

Blots Pen and Ink Supplies
14 Lyndhurst Avenue
Prestwich
Manchester M25 0GF
Tel: 0161 720 6916
www.blotspens.co.uk

Georgina Cowdrey
23 Oaklands Road
Petersfield
Hampshire GU32 2EY
Tel: 01730 300 816
Email: fg.cowdrey45@ntlworld.com

SAA (Society for All Artists)
PO Box 50
Newark
Nottinghamshire NG23 5GY
Tel: 01949 844 050
www.saa.co.uk/shop

London Graphic Centre
16–18 Shelton Street
London
WC2H 9JJ
Tel: 020 7759 4500
www.londongraphics.co.uk

Louisa Yuen Oriental Arts
5 Gardner Street
Brighton
East Sussex
BN1 1UP
Tel: 01273 819 168
Email:
louisayuen1000@yahoo.co.uk

INDEX

RELAXED TIGER
See pages 148–161 for instructions on painting animals with patterns.